THE RULES OF RES

THE RULES OF RESCUE

Cost, Distance, and Effective Altruism

Theron Pummer

OXFORD
UNIVERSITY PRESS

OXFORD
UNIVERSITY PRESS

Oxford University Press is a department of the University of Oxford. It furthers
the University's objective of excellence in research, scholarship, and education
by publishing worldwide. Oxford is a registered trade mark of Oxford University
Press in the UK and certain other countries.

Published in the United States of America by Oxford University Press
198 Madison Avenue, New York, NY 10016, United States of America.

Library of Congress Control Number: 2022029893

ISBN 978–0–19–088414–7

DOI: 10.1093/oso/9780190884147.001.0001

9 8 7 6 5 4 3 2 1
Printed by Sheridan Books, Inc., United States of America

To Hannah, Thomas, and Angus

CONTENTS

ACKNOWLEDGMENTS

For very helpful comments, I am grateful to Richard Arneson, Elizabeth Ashford, Ralf Bader, Adam Bales, Christian Barry, Saba Bazargan-Forward, Amy Berg, Brian Berkey, Joseph Bowen, David Brink, Mark Budolfson, Krister Bykvist, Timothy Campbell, Richard Yetter Chappell, Matthew Clark, Roger Crisp, Tyler Doggett, Romy Eskens, Cécile Fabre, Jessica Fischer, Johann Frick, Enrico Galvagni, Kerah Gordon-Solmon, Peter Graham, Jonas Harney, Joe Horton, Thomas Hurka, Michelle Hutchinson, Joel Joseph, Shelly Kagan, Frances Kamm, Benjamin Lange, Barry Maguire, Brian McElwee, Jeff McMahan, Per-Erik Milam, Kian Mintz-Woo, Andreas Mogensen, Daniel Muñoz, Oded Na'aman, Julia Nefsky, Dana Nelkin, Michael Otsuka, Douglas Portmore, Daniel Ramöller, Samuel Rickless, Tina Rulli, Benjamin Sachs, Andrea Sangiovanni, Thomas Schmidt, Thomas Sinclair, Peter Singer, Justin Snedegar, Luca Stroppa, Sarah Stroud, Larry Temkin, Sergio Tenenbaum, Johanna Thoma, Jordan Thomson, Travis Timmerman, Chris Tucker, Charlotte Unruh, Alec Walen, Fiona Woollard, Patrick Wu, Mingyang Xiao, Erik Zhang, and Robin Zheng. In addition, I would like to thank audiences at the London School of Economics; Princeton University; Purdue University; Queen's University; Rutgers University; Stockholm

University; Trinity College Dublin; University of California, Davis; University of California, San Diego; University of Cambridge; University of Edinburgh; University of Oxford; University of St Andrews; University of Toronto; University of Vermont; University of Warwick; University of York; and Yale University.

Some of the work in this book has been published before.

Chapter 1 (section 1.1), Chapter 2 (section 2.2), Chapter 3 (section 3.1), and Chapter 8 (section 8.3) each draw to some extent on, and Chapter 4 draws significantly on, Pummer 2021.

Chapter 3 (section 3.6) draws to some extent on Pummer 2019 and Muñoz and Pummer 2022.

Chapter 5 (sections 5.2 and 5.4) draws to some extent on Pummer and Crisp 2020.

INTRODUCTION

NON-CONSEQUENTIALISM AND METHODOLOGY

Is it wrong to let an innocent stranger die when you can rescue them at no cost? What if you could save either a few strangers or many others, at no cost to yourself either way—would it be wrong to save the few? Or what if, to save the lives of two strangers, you had to sacrifice your life, limbs, time, money, or personal projects—would it be wrong not to save them at such great costs to yourself? Is it ever wrong to save a few strangers at great cost to yourself rather than save many others at no greater cost to yourself?

These questions are clearly relevant to emergency rescue cases in which you can save more or fewer nearby people who are drowning, imperiled by hurtling boulders, or trapped in burning buildings. They are also relevant to constantly occurring cases in which you can use time or money to help distant people in need of food, shelter, or medical care. For example, by donating to charity, you can prevent distant strangers from dying of malaria. Depending on where you donate, you can provide more help or less.

This is a book about the moral reasons and requirements to use time, money, and other resources in ways that help others. I take it

The Rules of Rescue. Theron Pummer, Oxford University Press. © Oxford University Press 2023.
DOI: 10.1093/oso/9780190884147.003.0001

that you are not always morally required to provide the *most* help possible. First, there are moral *constraints* on doing so. You are not morally required to harvest an innocent non-consenting person's organs to save two others, just whenever this is what would help the most. You're morally required *not* to do that. Second, there are moral *permissions* not to help the most. You are not morally required to sacrifice your life to save two strangers, just whenever this is what would help the most. Had Edgar Wilson known he was going to drown in the River Thames while rescuing two boys, it would have been permissible not to jump in—such heroism is praiseworthy but beyond what is required.[1]

In accepting constraints and permissions, I'm rejecting *act consequentialism*, the view that you are always morally required to do whichever available act has the best outcome (I am likewise rejecting *act utilitarianism*, the view that you are always morally required to do whichever available act brings about the most well-being across all individuals). There are other versions of consequentialism, such as *rule consequentialism*. But since I doubt these other versions of consequentialism do much better in terms of accommodating constraints and permissions, I am drawn to *non-consequentialism* instead.[2]

Non-consequentialism isn't the view that consequences do not matter. It's just the view that consequences are not *all* that matter. Clearly, there are strong moral reasons to prevent significant harms from befalling strangers. It is morally wrong to allow these harms to occur when you could prevent them at no cost. Consequentialism does not have a monopoly on beneficence.

What is more, plausible versions of non-consequentialism hold that, in a range of cases, it is morally wrong not to prevent significant harms like suffering and death even when doing so involves incurring substantial personal costs. Plausible versions of non-consequentialism also hold that, in a range of cases, it is morally wrong to help a lesser number of strangers rather than comparably help a greater number of other strangers. I argue that these versions of non-consequentialism are not restricted to nearby emergency rescues but also apply to using time and money to help distant strangers (by volunteering, donating to charity, and making a difference with your career).

In earlier work, I argued that it is—in a significant range of cases—wrong to donate to less cost-effective charities rather than to more cost-effective charities, even when it is morally permissible not to donate (e.g., it's wrong to donate $6000 to a charity that on average saves one life per donation of this size, rather than donate $6000 to a charity that on average saves two lives per donation of this size, even when it's morally permissible not to donate this sum of money).[3] However, my argument took two important claims for granted: first, that it is wrong to save a lesser number of strangers rather than a greater number of other strangers and, second, that there are no relevant disanalogies between nearby rescue and distant rescue via charitable donation. In this book, I strengthen my previous argument by defending (qualified versions of) these claims. Moreover, it may seem paradoxical that it could be wrong to provide *some* help rather than *more* help when it's permissible to provide *no* help. I further strengthen my previous argument by dissolving apparent paradoxes generated by this claim.

Overall, this book is my attempt to articulate why each of us should be thinking about how to help more, whether by shifting our career, volunteering, or donating.[4] It is also an attempt to provide a defensible non-consequentialist picture of the moral reasons and requirements to engage in *effective altruism*, construed as the project of using time, money, and other resources to help others the most.[5] Clearly, act consequentialism supports engaging in effective altruism. But—contrary to the impression shared by many effective altruists and their critics alike—act consequentialism is only one of many very different moral views that support effective altruism. This matters for two reasons. First, most people reject act consequentialism. Whether or not effective altruism can find alternative philosophical support makes a difference to how many would be willing to join the cause. Second, act consequentialism is implausible. Effective altruism would lack plausible support if it lacked alternative support.

In providing a non-consequentialist picture of the moral reasons to use time, money, and other resources to help others the most, I do not present a fully formulated version of non-consequentialism as an alternative to act consequentialism's criterion of permissibility. Instead, I present my arguments within a *theoretically minimal* framework. This gives the arguments greater flexibility, allowing readers to fit them into their own favorite theories.

At various points throughout the book, I do endorse specific versions of non-consequentialism that I lean toward. But often this won't impact my main arguments or conclusions. For example, in Chapter 1, I defend "autonomy-based permitting reasons" in addition to "cost-based permitting reasons." And in Chapter 2, I suggest you're not required to toss a coin to determine which of two strangers to save (it is permissible just to save either, without first tossing a coin). Other non-consequentialists may reject autonomy-based permitting reasons or accept a requirement to toss a coin to determine which of two strangers to save. Readers who favor different versions of non-consequentialism can feel free to transpose my arguments from the point of departure, seeing where they lead. Many such variations can occur within the same broad picture according to which there are strong moral reasons to use time and money to help others the most.

Throughout the book, I appeal to intuitive claims about cases. Take the claim that you aren't morally required to harvest an innocent non-consenting person's organs just whenever this would have the best outcome. This is an *intuitive* claim in that it, considered independently, *seems* correct. We can find a claim intuitive without accepting it. For instance, an act consequentialist can agree that the above claim about the organs case is intuitive, even though they do not accept it. But it is a *price* of accepting act consequentialism that it is inconsistent with this intuitive claim (it is a further question whether it is worth paying the price to avoid other, greater ones).

Not all intuitive claims should be accommodated. Some intuitive claims can be debunked, particularly if they reflect biases or misunderstandings. Some intuitive claims are inconsistent with others so that at least one must be incorrect. Some are more intuitive than others. And some are found intuitive by a greater proportion of those who understand them.

What's more, accommodating intuitive claims about cases is not the only thing that matters when deciding between competing moral views. Suppose two views equally capture intuitive claims about cases, but whereas one view just consists of a list of these many claims, the other derives them from a few basic principles. *Parsimony* favors the latter view, with fewer unexplained elements. Or suppose both views derive all these intuitive claims from the same number of basic principles, but one view's principles are more intuitive *as principles* than the other view's principles. Intuitiveness at this more general level matters too.

Readers need not accept all the claims I've just made about intuitions. I invite those who disagree to approach the book with their own favored methodologies. The ways I rely on intuitive claims throughout the book are compatible with most approaches that aren't entirely dismissive of intuitions. And substantive moral views simply cannot be defended without relying on intuitions or judgments at *some* level.[6]

Many of the cases to which I appeal are imagined and thinly described. Consider the following case from Chapter 1:

Costly Rescue: A stranger faces a deadly threat. You can either do nothing, allowing them to die, or you can, at great cost to yourself, save their life.

When considering cases like this, complications beyond those mentioned are to be set aside. For example, the person you can rescue is an innocent, not a villain. They have a serious interest in staying alive. Saving them does not involve harming, lying, or stealing. Beyond losing your legs, there are no negative side effects of saving them. You are aware of all these details. We can suppose, for the sake of concrete illustration, that a boulder is hurtling toward the stranger. If you do nothing, it will crush them to death. You can save this person's life by putting your legs in the path of the boulder. There is no other way they can be saved.

Even when supplemented with this sort of concrete illustration, *Costly Rescue* remains rather stylized. I use clean cases like this for the same reason scientists use controlled experiments. In the real world, there are a lot of potentially relevant factors buzzing about. We need to minimize the "noise" introduced by factors other than those we're interested in testing. If we fail to control for confounding factors, it will remain unclear whether our experimental results are explained by the factor we were meant to be testing or instead by one or more of the factors correlated with it.

Were *Costly Rescue* more realistic, it would involve uncertainty about whether attempting to save the stranger by putting your legs in the path of the boulder would backfire, resulting in you or bystanders being crushed to death (along with the stranger). Such uncertainties could well make it seem morally permissible not to put your legs in the boulder's path to protect the stranger. But what we are trying to test with *Costly Rescue* is just whether you are morally required to incur a *great cost* (like the loss of your legs) when that would prevent a *much larger harm* (like death) from befalling a stranger. To consider the case properly, we need to make it somewhat unrealistic. We need to suppose you're sufficiently certain that putting your legs in the path of the boulder would save the stranger's life, crush your legs, and have no further "noteworthy" effects. Once we have controlled for confounding factors in this way, it may still seem you're morally permitted not to put your legs in the boulder's path to save the stranger. Then what we are finding intuitive is that a great cost to you can permit you not to save a stranger's life, even when it's much smaller than the harm of death. Other imagined cases used in this book are similarly controlled (see the Glossary of Cases).

Despite the advantages of using imagined cases, there are some dangers. One sort of danger is that an imagined case, used in an attempt to control for confounding factors in the real world, ends up introducing its own confounding factors. For example, many imagined cases in ethics involve victims being put in harm's way by diabolical agents, when there is an accidental or non-agential source of harm in purportedly analogous real-world cases. Many imagined cases resort to magic or science fiction, when this may blur our picture of what potentially relevant factors are present. But these dangers aren't reasons not to use imagined cases. They are reasons to *take care* when doing so. When using imagined cases, I try to avoid introducing confounds, and I try to make it easy for readers to get an imaginative grasp of what potentially relevant factors are present. Even if some of my cases are complicated, they are at least understandable.

In addition to these epistemic dangers of using imagined cases, there are dangers of practical inapplicability. The way two factors interact in the absence of other factors (in a "laboratory" setting) may differ from the way they interact in the presence of other factors (in "nature"). This can make it far from straightforward how to take the results of our controlled experiments and apply them to a messy world. Relatedly, in attempting to apply the lessons of thought experiments to the real world, we need to check the empirical details to make sure there is a reasonably good analogy between the designed case and the naturally occurring case in question. Ethicists may be so accustomed to thinking about ethically difficult problems in theory that they overlook ethically easy solutions in practice—there's no need to shove anyone in front of a runaway trolley to save many others, when you could instead just press the emergency stop button! Again, the remedy isn't to abandon imagined cases but to use them with care.

In sum, I frequently appeal to intuitive claims about imagined cases (as well as appeal to intuitive general claims or principles). I have addressed some concerns about the use of such cases, though I am afraid my brief remarks here won't convince those who are skeptical. I hope skeptics of the method of imagined cases can nonetheless get something out of the book.[7]

In a nutshell, then, here's the plan. Chapter 1 sets up the book's basic framework of reasons and how they serve to determine whether an act is required or permissible. Chapter 2 defends the intuitive claim that it is wrong to save a lesser number of strangers rather than a greater number of (at least twice as many) other strangers. Chapters 3 and 4 defend the claim that it can be wrong to save the lesser number rather than the greater number, even when it's permissible to save no one. These chapters dissolve two apparent paradoxes that are generated by this claim (Chapter 3 shows how the claim does not imply that if you are not going to save the greater number, then you are required to save no one; Chapter 4 shows how the claim allows that you can be praiseworthy for saving the lesser number, even when it is wrong to do so). The first four chapters defend a set of claims about the ethics of rescue in nearby emergencies. The remaining four chapters explore the extent to which these "rules of rescue" carry over to helping distant strangers by using time and money (assuming these resources rightfully belong to you). Chapter 5 shows how several differences between nearby rescue cases and distant rescue cases fail to capture the sense that it's wrong not to help in the former but permissible not to help in the latter.

Chapter 6 develops a view of how the frequency of opportunities to help over the course of your life affects reasons (not) to help on specific occasions. Chapter 7 turns to special connections, their ability to make it permissible or even required to save fewer people rather than more, and their interaction with considerations of frequency. Chapter 8 draws together the book's main argument: that core claims from Chapters 1–4, about requirements to help the most and permissions not to help the most, carry over to a significant range of real-world cases in which you can help using time and money. (This chapter includes a discussion of how to modify the book's main argument, when we drop the assumption that the time, money, and other resources in your possession rightfully belong to you.) It is argued that a significant proportion of us are required either to be effective altruists or else to provide no less help over our lives than we would have done if we did the minimum required as effective altruists.

More detailed chapter summaries can be found below.

Chapter 1: Requirements to Rescue and Permissions Not to

I introduce the book's basic framework of requiring reasons and permitting reasons. *Requiring reasons* serve to make acts required. *Permitting reasons* serve to make acts permissible (without serving to make acts required) by serving to prevent requiring reasons from making acts wrong. An act is required—wrong not to do—when there is most requiring reason overall to do it and no sufficiently strong permitting reason not to do it. A permitting reason is a kind of "defeater": when it's sufficiently strong, it prevents the balance of requiring reasons from making an act wrong. I then proceed to defend two main claims: first, that there are (strong) requiring reasons to rescue strangers from (large) harms and, second, that there are cost-based and autonomy-based permitting reasons not to rescue, which can make it permissible not to act in accord with the balance of requiring reasons to rescue. Taken together, these two claims explain how it can be wrong not to help in cases in which rescuing a stranger is costless to you (*Costless Rescue*) but permissible not to help in cases in which rescuing comes at great cost to you (*Costly Rescue*). Finally, I discuss the compatibility of these two claims with three competing views of rights to be rescued—the no-rights view, the cost-sensitive view, and the cost-insensitive view.

Chapter 2: Numbers Count

I defend a view about how the numbers count. First, I claim that (in *Costless No-Conflict*) it is wrong to save one stranger's life at no cost to yourself when you can instead save both this stranger's life *and* another's at no cost to yourself. I then defend the claim that (in *Costless Conflict*) it is wrong to save one stranger's life at no cost to yourself when you can instead save the lives of two other strangers at no cost to yourself. I defend a view of how the numbers count according to which there is nonetheless an important difference between conflict cases and no-conflict cases. While there is more requiring reason overall to save *A* and *C* than there is to save *A* (as in *Costless No-Conflict*) and more requiring reason overall to save *B* and *C* than there is to save *A* (as in *Costless Conflict*), there is an *individualist permitting reason* to save *A* in the latter case but not in the former case. While this individualist permitting reason to save *A* is not sufficiently strong to make it permissible to save *A* in this case, there is a sufficiently strong individualist permitting reason to save *A*'s life instead of saving *B*'s life and *C*'s *finger*. I further show that this view is compatible with the plausible claim that (in *Bored v. Joyful*) you are not required to save one stranger's life over another's just because the first stranger's remaining life would be of much higher quality than the second stranger's would be. And I show that this view of how the numbers count does not imply the counterintuitive "fully aggregative" claim that there is more requiring reason overall to save billions of people from very mild pain than there is to save one person from very intense agony.

Chapter 3: The All or Nothing Problem

I argue that (in *Costly No-Conflict*) it is wrong to save one stranger's life at great cost to yourself when you can instead save both this stranger's life and another's at the same great cost to yourself. This is so even when it is permissible to save neither stranger. There is a natural explanation of these claims. There is significantly more requiring reason overall to save the greater number than there is to do either alternative. But while there is a sufficiently strong permitting reason to do nothing, there is no sufficiently strong permitting reason to save the lesser number. I then turn to the "all or nothing problem" that the plausible claim that it is wrong to save the lesser number and the plausible claim that it is permissible to do nothing may together seem to imply the implausible claim that, if you are not going to save the greater number, you are required to do nothing. I present four possible solutions to this problem and reject all but one. According to my solution, although it is plain old wrong to save just one stranger, it can be *conditionally permissible* to do so—you may save just one *given that* you are not going to save both. I argue that my solution to the problem similarly applies to conflict cases (like *Costly Conflict*) in which you can save one stranger's life at great cost to yourself or instead save the lives of two other strangers at the same great cost to yourself.

Chapter 4: Praiseworthiness

I consider a new objection to the claim that (in cases like *Costly No-Conflict* and *Costly Conflict*) it is permissible to do nothing, wrong to save the lesser number, and permissible to save the greater number. The objection is that, if it is wrong to save the lesser number (and you lack an excuse for doing so), then you are overall blameworthy for saving the lesser number. But this is contrary to the intuition that (at least in *Costly Conflict*) you are worthy of *praise*, not blame, for heroically saving a stranger. In response, I argue that not all unexcused wrong acts are overall blameworthy, even if all are blameworthy to some extent. Some unexcused wrong acts are less responsive to the balance of requiring reasons than is required and yet seem overall praiseworthy (saving the lesser number in *Hand*). Other unexcused wrong acts are more responsive to the balance of requiring reasons than is required and yet seem overall praiseworthy (saving the lesser number in *Costly Conflict* and in *10 Plus Conflict*). Not only can you be praiseworthy overall for performing such wrong acts, but you can be *more* praiseworthy overall for performing such wrong acts than you would be for performing permissible alternatives.

Chapter 5: Distant Rescues

In *Pond*, you can save a drowning stranger at the cost of your new clothes. In *Charity*, you can donate to a malaria charity that saves on average one life for every $3000 they receive. In *Pond v. Charity*, you can either save a drowning stranger at the cost of your $6000 or instead donate this money to a malaria charity that saves on average one life for every $3000 they receive. Some argue that, due to one or more differences between cases like *Pond* and cases like *Charity*, it is wrong not to help in cases like *Pond*, permissible not to donate in cases like *Charity*, and permissible (if not also required) to help the drowning stranger in cases like *Pond v. Charity*. In this chapter, I focus on differences with respect to distance, salience, uniqueness, injustice, and diffusion. On the basis of several "clean" cases—which bracket various complications—I argue that these factors do not make the relevant sort of moral difference ("risky diffusion" is an exception). Whether taken individually or in combination, such factors would not make it the case that, while it is wrong not to help in cases like *Pond*, it is permissible not to donate in cases like *Charity*. Nor would they make

it the case that it is permissible to help the drowning stranger in
cases like *Pond v. Charity*.

Chapter 6: Frequent Rescues

While cases like *Pond* are rare, cases like *Charity* are very frequent. To isolate frequency, I examine *Frequent NearPlus*, a case in
which individual opportunities to help are like *Pond* with respect
to distance, salience, uniqueness, injustice, and diffusion—yet
arise very frequently. In this imagined case, it seems you are not
required to take every individual opportunity to help, even if you
are required to take some. I develop a view of requiring reasons
and permitting reasons that explains this plausible claim. The idea
behind this view is that "lifetime" features can amplify (cost-based
and autonomy-based) permitting reasons not to save strangers.
Crucially, it is the presence of permitting reasons that does the
explanatory work, rather than the absence of requiring reasons.
In *Frequent NearPlus*, there is an equally strong requiring reason
to save each stranger. I then turn to a variant of this case (*Rare/
Frequent NearPlus*), asking whether it can be permissible not to
respond to a frequently occurring opportunity to help even when
it would be wrong not to respond to an otherwise similar rarely
occurring opportunity to help. I argue that, while frequency cannot itself make this kind of moral difference, considerations of
cost and autonomy correlated with frequency can. Such considerations make it permissible to save the lesser number in a range of
cases like *Pond v. Charity*.

Chapter 7: Special Connections

The focus of this chapter is whether, when, and how special connections—including personal relationships, projects, and commitments—enhance requiring reasons or permitting reasons to save others. First, I look at some of the ways in which reasons can be enhanced by special connections, in accord with the kinds and degrees of these connections. Cases like *Pond* and *Charity* can differ with respect to special connections, as can different *Pond*-like rescues and different *Charity*-like rescues. Take a familiar real-world case in which you can donate to a charity to which you have a special connection or donate the same amount to a more cost-effective charity to which you have no special connection. Next, I show how lifetime features can amplify otherwise insufficiently strong permitting and requiring reasons to save a lesser number of people to whom you're specially connected over a greater number of strangers, making it permissible or even required to save the lesser number (I use *Frequent Friend v. Strangers* to show this). Finally, I distinguish between responsibly acquired special connections and non-responsibly acquired special connections and show how the former (but not the latter) can increase the cost you are required to incur in helping others over the course of your life.

Chapter 8: Must You Be an Effective Altruist?

I draw together the book's main argument: that core claims from Chapters 1–4, about requiring reasons to help the most and permitting reasons not to help the most, carry over to a significant range of real-world cases in which you can help using time and money. I argue that in the real world there is a *ubiquity of requiring reasons* to help strangers. This may seem overly demanding. I argue that it isn't, given that there's also a ubiquity of sufficiently strong permitting reasons. I then discuss how to modify the book's main argument, when we drop the assumption that the time, money, and other resources in your possession rightfully belong to you. Next, I define *effective altruism* as the project of using time, money, and other resources to help others the most; and I define an effective altruist as someone who engages in the project of effective altruism to a significant degree. Finally, I turn to whether you are required to be an effective altruist. I argue that a significant proportion of us are required either to be effective altruists or else to provide no less help over our lives than we would have done if we did the minimum required as effective altruists.

Notes

1. See   http://www.oxfordhistory.org.uk/streets/inscriptions/south_west/drowning.pdf.
2. For introductions to the contemporary debate between consequentialism and non-consequentialism, see Kagan 1998 (part 1) and Kamm 2007 (chapter 1). For defense of rule consequentialism as an alternative to act consequentialism, see Hooker 2000. For criticism of rule consequentialism and other sorts of indirect consequentialism, see Podgorski 2018. For an alternative view of the distinction between consequentialism and non-consequentialism, see Portmore forthcoming.
3. Pummer 2016a. For a reply, see Sinclair 2018.

4. If you're considering taking action, I'd recommend starting with https://80000hours.org/ for careers and https://www.givewell.org/ or https://funds.effectivealtruism.org/ for donations.

5. For an introduction to effective altruism, see https://www.effectivealtruism.org/ and MacAskill 2015. Also see MacAskill 2019a and MacAskill and Pummer 2020 on the definition of effective altruism.

6. On the role of intuitions in ethics, see McMahan 2000, Huemer 2005, Singer 2005, Appiah 2008 (chapter 3), Brink 2014, Harman 2015, Crisp 2015 (chapter 4), Chappell 2015, McGrath 2019, and Stratton-Lake 2020.

7. On the role of cases in ethics, see Kagan 2001, Elster 2011, Fried 2012, Kamm 2013 (chapter 27), Burri 2020, and Slavny et al. 2021. On intuitions about emergency rescues, see Barry and Øverland 2013, Haydar and Øverland 2019, Thomson 2020, and Sterri and Moen 2021. On intuitions about sacrificing limbs, see Barry and Øverland 2013, Barnes 2016, and Lippert-Rasmussen 2019.

1 | REQUIREMENTS TO RESCUE AND PERMISSIONS NOT TO

1.1. Requirements and Permissions

Consider the following case:

> *Costless Rescue*: A stranger faces a deadly threat. You can either do nothing, allowing them to die, or you can, at no cost to yourself, save their life.

Complications beyond those mentioned are set aside. The person you can rescue is an innocent, not a villain. They have a serious interest in staying alive. Saving them does not involve harming, lying, or stealing. There are no negative side effects of saving them. You are aware of all these details.

Suppose, for the sake of concrete illustration, that a boulder is hurtling toward a stranger. If you do nothing, it will crush them to death. You can save this person's life by effortlessly kicking a

The Rules of Rescue. Theron Pummer, Oxford University Press. © Oxford University Press 2023.
DOI: 10.1093/oso/9780190884147.003.0002

log into the path of the boulder. There is no other way they can be saved.

You are morally required to save the stranger. It is morally impermissible—that is, wrong—to let them die. I henceforth largely omit the word "morally," but this is the sort of requirement and permissibility I have in mind throughout the book.

Next consider:

> *Costly Rescue*: A stranger faces a deadly threat. You can either do nothing, allowing them to die, or you can, at great cost to yourself, save their life.

Depending on how great this cost to you is, it can be permissible—that is, not wrong—to allow the stranger to die. Surely it is permissible to let a stranger die when saving them costs you your own life. But it also seems permissible to let a stranger die when saving them costs you much less than this. You have a permission not to save a stranger when this comes at a great cost to you, even if not saving the stranger comes at a much greater cost to them.[1]

Suppose, for the sake of concrete illustration, that a boulder is again hurtling toward a stranger. If you do nothing, it will crush them to death. You can save this person's life by putting your legs in the path of the boulder. There is no other way they can be saved. Losing your legs in this way is very painful and disruptive—it's a substantial cost. I take it that this cost is great enough to make it permissible to let a stranger die.

What kinds of cost can make it permissible not to help? There are many things besides life and limb that might be sacrificed in the course of helping strangers. For instance, time, comfort, effort, safety, and money. I take it that costs with respect to these various things can also make it permissible not to help. Nonetheless, not all kinds of cost can make it permissible not to help. Feeling disgusted at the thought of rescuing someone with dark skin cannot make it permissible not to rescue them (racist disgust is not a cost that can permit not helping, if it is a cost at all). For another example, suppose you steal my money, and now I need it back to pay my bills. It would seem outrageous that the cost to you of returning my money could make it permissible to keep it for yourself.[2]

In addition, it is not clear that all kinds of *help* can generate requirements. It seems you can be required to prevent losses that are significantly painful or disruptive. And it seems you can be required to provide gains that meet basic needs for food, shelter, and medical care. But it is not clear that you can be required to provide gains for strangers who are already sufficiently well off (if such gains can require you to help, it would seem they can do so only when they are disproportionately large). Plausibly the first two kinds of help involve *preventing significant harm*, while the third involves *providing pure benefit*; but what matters here is that the first two kinds of help can generate requirements, while it is not clear the third kind can.[3]

I largely sidestep questions of what kinds of cost can permit you not to help and what kinds of help can generate requirements. Instead, I focus on cases in which help and costs are relatively uncontroversially of the relevant kinds.

Which costs over the course of your life can make it permissible not to help on a given occasion? Is it only the cost of helping *on that occasion*, or is it that cost plus the total *lifetime cost* you will have independently incurred while helping strangers? I return to this question in Chapter 6. Until then, it can be useful to suppose that the rescue situations in question occur very rarely, and indeed take place in an imaginary world in which your opportunities to help are very rare (so that the lifetime cost of helping is never much greater than the cost of helping in one of these rare rescue situations).

How great must the cost to you be to make it permissible not to help strangers? That depends, among other things, on how much your sacrifice would help. For example, it might be permissible not to save a stranger's foot when that costs you your finger. It might nonetheless be wrong not to save a stranger's life when that costs you your finger.

On one view, you are permitted not to help strangers when that comes at a cost to you, unless the help they receive is at least M times greater than the cost to you.[4] It is uncertain how large this multiplier M can reasonably be. There may even be no precise fact of the matter. Defenders of this view can nonetheless argue that M mustn't be too large or too small. It cannot be so large that their view implies it is permissible not to save a stranger's life when the only cost to you of saving their life is scratching your finger. M cannot be so small that the view implies it is wrong to allow a stranger to suffer 100 headaches when the cost to you of preventing them is suffering 99 equally bad headaches.

However, it might prove impossible to find a fixed multiplier M, suitable for all cases. For example, it may seem you are required to prevent a stranger from suffering 100 headaches when the cost to you is suffering one equally bad headache. This would suggest an M of less than 100. Still, it may seem permissible not to prevent a stranger from suffering 100 years of agony when the cost to you is suffering one year of equally intense agony. This would suggest an M of at least 100. So perhaps M can vary in accordance with the cost to you of helping strangers.

Some hold the view that, if the cost to you of helping strangers is sufficiently large, it is permissible not to incur this cost, no matter how much it would help these strangers.[5] It is a bit shocking and disturbing to suppose that you could be required to pay *any* enormous cost for strangers, as long as their need is great enough. Could you really be required to help them at the cost of your life, years of intense suffering, or both? We avoid these counterintuitive implications if we accept the view that there is an absolute limit on how much cost you can be required to incur in the course of helping strangers.

But this view faces its own difficulties. It has the counterintuitive implication that there is a radical difference between incurring a sufficiently large cost and incurring a somewhat smaller cost.[6] Suppose, for example, that the absolute limit on how much cost you can be required to incur is roughly one year of pain, so that 360 days is definitely under the limit and 370 days is definitely over the limit. The view could then imply that, while you are required to save the lives of 1000 strangers when the cost to you is 360 days of pain, you are permitted not to save *billions* when the cost to you is 370 days of pain. Though this implication is counterintuitive, it's not clearly worse than those we face if we do not accept some such absolute limit view. At any rate, it is not my aim here to resolve the debate between absolute limit views and multiplier views.

Even if we are quite unsure about how great the cost to you must be to make it permissible not to help strangers, there remains a fair bit about which we can be confident. For instance, you are required to prevent strangers from suffering significant harms—including relatively modest harms like sprained ankles—when this comes at no cost to you whatsoever. You are required to save the lives of strangers when this comes at significant but relatively modest cost to you. And you are *not* required to save the life of a stranger when the cost to you is great enough, even if it's much less than death.

While the harm you can prevent serves to require you to rescue, the cost to you of rescuing serves to permit you not to. Throughout this book, I adopt a basic framework of *requiring reasons* (considerations that serve to require) and *permitting reasons* (considerations that serve to permit without serving to require). Here are more precise definitions of these key terms.

A *requiring reason* to do an act *A* contributes toward making *A* required. A requiring reason to do an act does not always make it required. After all, there may be a stronger requiring reason to do an alternative *B*—pulling with greater force in another direction—so that there is *more requiring reason overall* to do *B* than there is to do *A*. For example, there is a requiring reason not to shove me onto the ground. But there is a stronger requiring reason to prevent a stranger from being killed by a boulder. If the only way to prevent the stranger from being killed involves shoving me onto the ground, then there is more requiring reason overall to shove me to the ground than to refrain. I will take it that an act *A* is *wrong* when there is more requiring reason overall to do an alternative *B* than there is to do A and no sufficiently strong permitting reason to do A. And an act A is *required* when there is most requiring reason overall to do A and no sufficiently strong permitting reason to do an alternative B.

A *permitting reason* to do an act A contributes toward making A permissible *without* also contributing toward making A required. It pulls toward permissibility indirectly: when there is more requiring reason overall to do alternative B than there is to do A, a permitting reason to do A (rather than B) would *contribute toward preventing* this fact from making A wrong. A permitting reason is thus a kind of "defeater": when it's sufficiently strong, it prevents the balance of requiring reasons from making an act wrong.

Permitting reasons as I construe them are importantly structurally different from requiring reasons. While the requiring reasons (count noun) to do an act can be "weighed up" to yield the overall requiring reason (mass noun) to do an act, permitting reasons do not similarly weigh up to yield overall permitting reason. Instead, permitting reasons to do A always take the form of pairwise comparisons with each of the alternatives to A. Here is the idea. For each alternative to A, check whether there is more requiring reason overall to do it than there is to do A. If there are some alternatives that there is more requiring reason overall to do than there is to do A, then, for each such alternative B, check whether there is a sufficiently strong permitting reason to do A rather than B. If, for each such alternative B there is a sufficiently strong permitting reason to do A rather than B, then A is permissible. But if, for any such alternative B, there is no sufficiently strong permitting reason to do A rather than B, then A is wrong. If there are no alternatives that there is more requiring reason overall to do than there is to do *A*, then *A* is permissible. When an act is in this way supported by the balance of requiring reasons, no permitting reason is needed for the act to be permissible. Or, if you prefer, a permitting reason of zero strength would be sufficient.[7]

There is a requiring reason to save the stranger in *Costless Rescue*. There is an equivalent requiring reason in *Costly Rescue*. However, while there is no sufficiently strong permitting reason not to save the stranger in *Costless Rescue*, there is a sufficiently strong permitting reason not to save the stranger in *Costly Rescue*. In *Costly Rescue*, the cost to you of saving the stranger is not a scratched finger or stubbed toe. Such a small cost might provide you with a weak permitting reason not to save the stranger, but it would clearly be an insufficiently strong permitting reason next to the strong requiring reason to save the stranger's life. In *Costly Rescue*, saving the stranger comes at the cost of painfully losing your legs. I take it that is a sufficiently strong permitting reason, even next to the strong requiring reason to save the stranger's life. You are permitted, but not required, to refrain from helping (setting aside such complications as costs to others of you losing your legs). This is not to deny that you are *prudentially* required to keep your legs. I doubt there is a *morally* requiring reason to keep your legs, but even if there is, there is more morally requiring reason overall to save the stranger at the cost of your legs than there is to do nothing. But for all that you are not morally required to incur this cost since there is a sufficiently strong morally permitting reason to keep your legs.

Again, I largely omit the word "morally" throughout the book, but I have in mind moral requirement, moral permissibility, morally requiring reasons, morally permitting reasons, and so on, unless otherwise specified.

1.2. Cost and Autonomy

So far I have focused on how costs to you of helping strangers can make it permissible not to help. Sacrifices of limbs, comfort, safety, time, and money can give rise to cost-based permitting reasons not to help. But, as I have noted, not all costs can make it permissible not to help. In addition, it is plausible that not all permitting reasons are cost-based. Arguably there are non-cost-based permitting reasons capable of making it permissible not to help even when helping comes at no cost to you.

Suppose that a stranger urgently needs a kidney transplant to live and that you are the only match. If the cost to you of giving this stranger your kidney were great enough, it would be permissible not to do so (this would be another instance of *Costly Rescue*). But suppose that giving up your kidney comes at very little cost to you. You accordingly have at most a weak cost-based permitting reason not to give it to the stranger in need. At the same time, there is a strong requiring reason to save this stranger. So, if all permitting reasons are cost-based, you are in such a case required to give away your kidney to save the stranger's life.

Defenders of the view that all permitting reasons are cost-based may be prepared to accept this conclusion, even if it is counterintuitive. But this may be too counterintuitive to accept. We can avoid such conclusions if we hold that there are permitting reasons to determine your own life. Call such permitting reasons *autonomy-based* permitting reasons. Such permitting reasons can be present even in the absence of costs, and they reflect a margin of moral "breathing room," a space of meaningful alternatives shielded from moral requirements.[8] It is plausible that such permitting reasons are stronger, the bigger the difference your choice makes to how your life unfolds. Think of big choices like what career to pursue, where to live, and whether and whom to marry. Suppose that you would save many more lives as a philanthropist banker than as a humanitarian doctor. Even if it would also be better *for you* to be a banker, you could still have a sufficiently strong autonomy-based permitting reason to be a doctor—after all, your choice of career may well determine how you spend 80,000 hours of your life.[9]

It does not seem plausible that there are autonomy-based permitting reasons to act in ways that contravene the rights of others, by harming them or using what rightfully belongs to them without their consent. By contrast, it seems plausible that there can be cost-based permitting reasons to act in ways that contravene the rights of others. For example, it would seem permissible to roll a boulder onto a stranger's hand—contravening their right not to be harmed—were this a necessary side effect of preventing the boulder from crushing you to death. But it seems that, setting costs aside, your moral breathing room cannot plausibly include contravening the rights of others.

Even when autonomy-based permitting reasons are present, they will not always be sufficiently strong. To see this, suppose that a stranger is having a heart attack and needs aspirin to live. You can reach into your bag and hand them some of the aspirin that is rightfully yours. It costs you next to nothing to hand them your aspirin, there is no one else around, and there are no other complicating factors. Clearly you are required to hand over your aspirin and thereby save the stranger's life. The fact that the aspirin is rightfully yours does not imply that you are permitted to use it as you choose but does imply that there's an autonomy-based permitting reason (of *some* strength) to use it as you choose. If there were only a very weak requiring reason to give the stranger your aspirin, it could be permissible to refuse to give it to them. But they need the aspirin to live. The autonomy-based permitting reason to keep your aspirin is not sufficiently strong next to the strong requiring reason to save the stranger's life.

The requiring reason to save the stranger is as strong in the kidney case as it is in the aspirin case. And while there is clearly not a sufficiently strong permitting reason to keep your aspirin, it is plausible that there is a sufficiently strong permitting reason to keep your kidney. What could explain this difference?

One putative explanation is that your kidney is part of your body. We might argue that there is a stronger autonomy-based permitting reason to determine your own life when this involves the use of your body than when it involves the use of external resources such as your aspirin, clothes, or car. But what if you could save a life by painlessly popping out a vital organ and handing it to the surgeon while instantly regenerating a perfectly functional new one, just as simply and easily as handing over an aspirin? Or what if all that's needed to save a stranger is a hair plucked from your head? In these imagined cases, it is not plausible that there remains a sufficiently strong autonomy-based permitting reason not to hand over your body part. This suggests that the fact that your kidney is part of your body does not explain why there would be a sufficiently strong autonomy-based permitting reason not to hand over your kidney but no such permitting reason not to hand over your aspirin.

A better explanation is that more of your life stands to be determined in the kidney case than in the aspirin case. Whether or not you go ahead with a kidney transplant operation typically makes a significant difference to how your life unfolds for a non-trivial length of time. Among other things, going ahead with such an operation involves a trip to the hospital and being wheeled into an operating room, not to mention recovery time. Even if the operation's downsides were balanced by its upsides so that you'd be better off overall for having had it—and even if there were no downsides at all—whether you go ahead with the kidney operation could still make a significant difference to what activities your life will contain over a nontrivial length of time. This would seem enough to trigger a significant autonomy-based permitting reason not to go ahead with the operation. In the aspirin case, the only significant difference between your alternatives is whether the stranger lives or dies. It is accordingly not plausible that there is a significant autonomy-based permitting reason not to hand over your aspirin.

1.3. Rights to Be Rescued

Consider two main claims I have defended: first, that there are (strong) requiring reasons to rescue strangers from (large) harms and, second, that there are permitting reasons not to rescue, which can make it permissible not to act in accord with the balance of requiring reasons to rescue.

In this section, I discuss the compatibility of these two claims with three competing views of when those in need of rescue have *moral rights* to be rescued. On the *no-rights* view, there are no rights to be rescued. On the *cost-sensitive* view, there are rights to be rescued at little or no cost but not at great cost. And on the *cost-insensitive* view, there are rights to be rescued even at great cost.[10] Readers who are unconcerned with this debate about rights can skip this section.

In general, when someone has a right that you (not) perform some act A, you owe it to them that you (not) do A. Failing to (not) do A contravenes their right. If you contravene this person's right, you owe them compensation for doing so, other things being equal. You can owe them compensation for contravening their right even when it is permissible to contravene their right (sometimes the government or other third parties may owe the victim compensation, rather than the agent who permissibly contravened the right). In addition, third parties may be permitted to forcibly prevent you from contravening this person's right, at least when it's wrong to contravene it.

Consider rights not to be harmed. Suppose you deliberately roll a boulder onto an innocent stranger's hand, thereby crushing it. This contravenes their right that you not cause them significant harm. As a result of your act, you owe them compensation. If you could give a prosthetic hand to this person or to a stranger who lost their hand in an earthquake, you would, other things being equal, be required to give the prosthetic hand to the person whose hand you crushed. (Cases of contravening a right to be rescued by letting someone die raise the difficult question of how to compensate the victim; if compensating a deceased victim is impossible, perhaps the next best thing is to advance their personal projects posthumously or to compensate their nearest and dearest.) It seems you would still owe the stranger compensation even if you crushed their hand *permissibly*, say, as a necessary side effect of preventing the boulder from killing you.

Now consider rights to be rescued. Suppose a boulder is hurtling toward a stranger's hand. If you do nothing, it will crush their hand. You can save this person's hand by effortlessly kicking a log into the path of the boulder. There is no other way their hand can be saved. It is wrong not to save their hand. But would you owe them compensation if you failed to save their hand? If, at some point after allowing their hand to be crushed, you could give them a prosthetic hand or instead give it to a stranger who lost their hand in an earthquake, would you, other things being equal, be required to give the prosthetic hand to the stranger whose hand you allowed to be crushed? The no-rights view implies you wouldn't be, while the cost-sensitive view and the cost-insensitive view each imply you would be. Were it sufficiently costly to save the stranger's hand—say, were it to cost you your finger—the cost-sensitive view implies you wouldn't owe them compensation for failing to save their hand.

Suppose the no-rights view is correct. Then, even in cases in which saving a stranger's hand is costless to you, they lack a right that you save their hand. It is nonetheless clear that, in such cases, there is most requiring reason overall to save their hand. Since there is no sufficiently strong permitting reason not to save their hand, you are required to do so. Similarly, even if in *Costless Rescue* the stranger whose life you can save lacks a right that you save their life, you are required to do so. If the no-rights view is correct, then it can be wrong not to rescue a stranger even though they have no right that you do so.

Alternatively, suppose the cost-sensitive view of rights to be rescued is correct. Then a stranger can have a right that you save their hand when this costs you nothing but lack a right that you save their hand when this costs you your finger. Even in cases like the latter, it is nonetheless clear that there is most requiring reason overall to save their hand. The cost of your finger can be a sufficiently strong permitting reason not to save their hand, and it can make it the case that you would not owe the stranger compensation for failing to save their hand. But the cost of your finger cannot plausibly remove the requiring reason to save the stranger's hand. Similarly, even if in *Costly Rescue* the stranger whose life you can save lacks a right that you save their life, there is most requiring reason overall to do so. If this cost-sensitive view of rights is correct, then there can be most requiring reason overall to rescue a stranger even though they have no right that you do so.

Finally, the cost-insensitive view is clearly compatible with the claim that there are requiring reasons to rescue strangers in the costless and costly variants of the hand-rescue case (and in *Costless Rescue* and *Costly Rescue*). Regardless of the cost to you, those you can rescue have rights to be rescued, and there are requiring reasons to do so. But again, the cost to you can make it permissible not to rescue a stranger. So, if the cost-insensitive view of rights is correct, then it can be permissible not to rescue a stranger even though they have a right that you do so.

Whichever of these three competing views of rights to be rescued is correct, the first main claim I have defended—that there are (strong) requiring reasons to rescue strangers from (large) harms—remains plausible. Let's turn to the second main claim I have defended, that there are cost-based and autonomy-based permitting reasons not to rescue, which can make it permissible not to act in accord with the balance of requiring reasons to rescue.

First consider cost-based permitting reasons. That it would cost you your finger is a sufficiently strong permitting reason not to save a stranger's hand. This is clearly compatible with the claim that the stranger lacks a right that you save their hand (as implied by the no-rights view and the cost-sensitive view). It is also compatible with the claim that the stranger *has* a right that you save their hand (as implied by the cost-insensitive view). While the cost to you of saving the stranger's hand is a sufficiently strong permitting reason not to save their hand, you could nonetheless owe the stranger compensation for contravening their right that you save their hand. Similar remarks apply to *Costly Rescue*.

Now consider autonomy-based permitting reasons, that is, permitting reasons to determine your own life without contravening the rights of others. If someone has a right that you save them from harm, then failing to save them contravenes their right. So, when someone has a right that you save them, there is no autonomy-based permitting reason not to do so.

The cost-sensitive view and the cost-insensitive view each imply that there is no autonomy-based permitting reason not to save a heart attack victim's life by giving them your aspirin when this comes at little cost to you. After all, these views imply that this person has a right that you give them your aspirin. These views similarly imply that there is no autonomy-based permitting reason not to give your kidney to a stranger who needs it to live, when giving up your kidney comes at little cost to you.

But it seems plausible that if going ahead with the kidney operation makes a significant difference to what activities your life will contain over a sufficient length of time, then—even when giving up your kidney comes at little cost to you—there is a sufficiently strong autonomy-based permitting reason not to give up your kidney. Since there couldn't be an autonomy-based permitting reason not to save someone who has a right that you save them, it must be that the stranger who needs your kidney does not have a right that you save them.

In this way the kidney case casts some doubt on both the cost-sensitive view and the cost-insensitive view. But even if we should reject these views, it would not follow that we should accept the no-rights view. The heart attack victim may still have a right that you give them your aspirin, even if rights to be rescued are restricted so that a stranger lacks a right to be rescued by you when rescuing them makes a significant difference to what activities your life will contain over a sufficient length of time (as in the kidney case). Perhaps strangers lack rights to be rescued by you when this makes such a substantial difference to how your life unfolds. Rather than accept the no-rights view, we could accept a restricted version of the cost-sensitive view or the cost-insensitive view.

In this section I have discussed the compatibility of this chapter's two main claims with three competing views of rights to be rescued. The two main claims are that there are (strong) requiring reasons to rescue strangers from (large) harms and that there are cost-based and autonomy-based permitting reasons not to rescue.

The three competing views of rights to be rescued are the no-rights view, the cost-sensitive view, and the cost-insensitive view. The two claims are compatible with each of the three views, with the exception that the cost-sensitive view and the cost-insensitive view are each incompatible with autonomy-based permitting reasons not to rescue. But these views of rights can be restricted to achieve compatibility with autonomy-based permitting reasons.

Notes

1. On permissions, see Parfit 1978, Scheffler 1982, Kagan 1989, Quong 2009, Hurka and Shubert 2012, and Lazar 2019. Permissions are standardly thought to be "agent-relative." They make it permissible for you not to incur a great cost to *yourself*, thereby allowing a stranger to bear a much greater cost. But they don't make it permissible to prevent a great cost to a *stranger*, thereby allowing another stranger to bear a much greater cost. For an agent-neutral account of permissions, see Frowe 2021.

2. On what kinds of cost can permit not helping, see Barry and Lawford-Smith 2019. On differences between "cost" and "difficulty," see Woollard 2016 and McElwee 2016.

3. On harm, see Shiffrin 1999, Harman 2009, Shiffrin 2012, Bradley 2012, and Rabenberg 2014. For skepticism about requirements to help, see Sachs 2017 (chapter 8).

4. Scheffler's 1982 "agent-centered prerogative" is a prominent example of this sort of view.

5. See Cullity 2004, Hooker 2009, Stroud 2013, and Frick unpublished.

6. Such "radical difference" issues are importantly distinct from "precise cutoff" issues (such as the issue for multiplier views of how large the multiplier M can reasonably be). For discussion, see Pummer 2022 and Pummer forthcoming.

7. The distinction between requiring reasons and permitting reasons is inspired by Gert 2003 and 2016, who distinguishes between a reason's "requiring strength" and its "justifying strength." Those who wish to maintain something closer to Gert's official picture can translate "requiring reasons" and "permitting reasons" in terms of the requiring strength and permitting strength of a reason. This will not affect the main arguments of the book. (Also note that Gert's focus is rational permissibility, whereas mine is moral permissibility.)

Requiring reasons or similar have been around in the literature for quite some time—for example, they can be likened to Rossian "prima facie duties," though note that Ross 1930 (20) himself apologizes for the misleading phrase "prima facie" as he intends to be referring not to appearances but to actual features that play a contributory role in the determination of all things considered duties.

Permitting reasons are a more recent addition—see Parfit 1978, Scheffler 1982, Portmore 2008, Hurka and Shubert 2012, and Muñoz 2021. I take permitting reasons to be "defeaters" or "disablers" (Dancy 2004) that serve to prevent the balance of requiring reasons from making acts wrong. Others take permitting reasons to be considerations that directly serve to make acts permissible without serving to make them required (Hurka and Shubert 2012 and Hurka and Tsagarakis 2021). I suspect my construal is preferable on grounds of parsimony, but the latter construal can be adopted without affecting the book's main arguments. Notice also the contrastive nature of permitting reasons as I construe them—they (indirectly) serve to permit you to do one alternative *rather than* another. When there is more requiring reason overall to do A than there is to do C and more requiring reason overall to do B than there is to do C, then a sufficiently strong permitting reason to do C rather than B is not enough to make C permissible. What's also needed is a sufficiently strong permitting reason to do C rather than A. See Snedegar 2017 for an account of contrastivism about reasons, and see Muñoz 2021 on contrastive prerogatives.

8. On autonomy-based considerations broadly of this sort, see Shiffrin 1991, Kamm 1992, Woollard 2015, Lazar 2019, and Fischer unpublished. For criticism, see Kagan 1989 (223–241) and Arneson 2004.

9. On making a difference with your career, see Buss 2006 and https://800
   00hours.org/.

10. See Thomson 1971 (60–61) and 1990 (160–161) for defense of the no-
    rights view. See Feinberg 1984 (chapter 4) and Frowe 2019 (211 and
    footnote 22) for defense of the cost-sensitive view. See Sinclair 2018
    (section VI) for defense of the cost-insensitive view. On the enforceability
    of rights to be rescued, see Malm 1995, Fabre 2002, and Bowen
    unpublished. For more general discussions of rights, see Hohfeld 1913
    and Kamm 2007 (chapters 7–9).

2 | NUMBERS COUNT

2.1. Differences in Number

In the previous chapter, I introduced the book's basic framework of requiring reasons and permitting reasons. *Requiring reasons* serve to make acts required. *Permitting reasons* serve to make acts permissible (without serving to make acts required) by serving to prevent requiring reasons from making acts wrong. An act is required when there is most requiring reason overall to do it and no sufficiently strong permitting reason not to do it. A permitting reason—which is a kind of defeater—is sufficiently strong when it prevents the balance of requiring reasons from making an act wrong. In the previous chapter, I defended two main claims: first, that there are (strong) requiring reasons to rescue strangers from (large) harms and, second, that there are cost-based and autonomy-based permitting reasons not to rescue, which can make it permissible not to act in accord with the balance of requiring reasons to rescue. In this chapter, I turn to cases in which you can rescue different *numbers* of people.

The Rules of Rescue. Theron Pummer, Oxford University Press. © Oxford University Press 2023.
DOI: 10.1093/oso/9780190884147.003.0003

Consider the following case:

Costless No-Conflict: Two strangers face a deadly threat. You can
do nothing, save one stranger's life at no cost to yourself, or save
both their lives at no cost to yourself.

As before, complications beyond those mentioned are set aside.
Those you can rescue are innocents, not villains. They have serious
interests in staying alive. Saving them does not involve harming,
lying, or stealing. You are aware of all these details.

Suppose, for the sake of concrete illustration, that a boulder is
hurtling toward one stranger and that another boulder is hurtling
toward another stranger. If you do nothing, both strangers will
be crushed to death. You can save one life by effortlessly kicking
a shorter log into the path of one of the boulders. You can instead
save both lives by effortlessly kicking a longer log into the path of
both boulders. There is no other way either person can be saved.

You are required to save both strangers. It is impermissible—
that is, wrong—to let them both die. It is also wrong to save just
one. In *Costless No-Conflict*, there is a strong requiring reason to
save each stranger and more requiring reason overall to save both
than to save just one. There is most requiring reason overall to save
the lives of both strangers and no sufficiently strong permitting
reason not to. So, it is wrong not to save both.

That it is wrong not to save both strangers in *Costless No-
Conflict* shows that the number of people helped is morally relevant in at least the following sense: it is wrong not to prevent
additional strangers from suffering significant harm when there is

no reason to do otherwise. The amount of help provided for each person is similarly morally relevant: it is wrong not to prevent a stranger from suffering significantly greater harm when there is no reason to do otherwise. For example, suppose you can at no cost to yourself either way save a stranger's left arm only or instead save both of their arms. It is wrong not to save both of their arms.

Next consider:

> *Costless Conflict*: Three strangers face a deadly threat. You can do nothing, save one stranger's life at no cost to yourself, or save the other two at no cost to yourself. Tragically, you cannot save all three.

Suppose, for the sake of concrete illustration, that a boulder to your left is hurtling toward one stranger and that a boulder to your right is hurtling toward two other strangers. If you do nothing, all three strangers will be crushed to death. You can save the one stranger by effortlessly kicking a log to your left. You can instead save the other two by effortlessly kicking a log to your right.

In both *Costless Conflict* and *Costless No-Conflict*, you can save the lives of two strangers or instead save the life of one stranger. But there is an important difference between these cases. In *Costless No-Conflict*, requiring reasons do not conflict. There is a requiring reason to save stranger A and a requiring reason to save stranger B. Saving both A and B responds to both reasons. In *Costless Conflict*, requiring reasons conflict. There is a requiring reason to save stranger A, a requiring reason to save stranger B, and a requiring reason to save stranger C. You cannot respond to all these reasons. This fact about conflict cases forces us to ask whether and how these conflicting reasons *balance* against each other. (A similar point holds for conflict cases involving different amounts of help for each, as when you can either save only the left arm of one stranger or instead save both arms of another stranger.)

Most of us find it wrong to save the lesser number in cases like *Costless Conflict*, despite the conflict between requiring reasons. It seems plausible that there is more requiring reason overall to save *B* and *C* than there is to save *A* and that there is no sufficiently strong permitting reason to save *A*. In the rest of this chapter, I defend the claim that it is wrong to save the lesser number in conflict cases.

2.2. What Makes It Wrong to Save the Lesser Number in Conflict Cases

In cases like *Costless Conflict* there are three alternatives, "save no one," "save *A*," and "save *B* and *C*," and all else is equal. Saving the greater number has the best outcome. Is this what makes it wrong to save the lesser number?

According to *act consequentialism*, you are always morally required to do whichever available act has the best outcome. This view has the implausible implication that you are required to harvest an innocent non-consenting person's organs to save others whenever this is the available act that has the best outcome (even when refraining from doing so has an only marginally suboptimal outcome). It is not plausible that you are required to do what has the best outcome, regardless of the moral constraints this would violate—such as constraints against harming, lying, or stealing. And, as noted in the previous chapter, it is plausible that there are moral permissions: you are not required to save the life of a stranger at the cost of your legs, even if that would produce much the best outcome (*Costly Rescue*).

One possibility is to restrict the requirement to promote the best outcome so that it applies only when constraints and permissions don't. But even then it is not clear that you are required to do what has the best outcome. Suppose you can either do nothing or at no cost to yourself give a sufficiently well-off stranger a piece of candy. Of your alternatives, giving the stranger the candy would make things go best. However, it is not clear that you are *required* to do this. There are requiring reasons to prevent strangers from suffering significant harms, including such relatively modest harms as sprained ankles and lost fingers; but it is not clear that there are requiring reasons to provide (small) pure benefits to sufficiently well-off strangers.[1] Or suppose that saving one stranger's life would produce a slightly better outcome than saving another stranger's life would. It seems plausible that you are permitted to save either (or required to toss a coin).

According to another view, the fact that saving one stranger's (*A*'s) life is morally equivalent to saving another stranger's (*B*'s) life is what makes it wrong to save the lesser number in cases like *Costless Conflict*. Since it is wrong to save *A*'s life instead of saving *A*'s life and *C*'s life (in *Costless No-Conflict*) and since saving *A*'s life is morally equivalent to saving *B*'s life, it is wrong to save *A*'s life instead of saving *B*'s life and *C*'s life (in *Costless Conflict*).[2]

But this is not correct. The fact that when you can save A's life or B's life you are permitted to save either (or required to toss a coin) does not show that saving A is morally equivalent to saving B in the way assumed above. It is true that, whether you save A or save B, you save exactly one person. But reasons to rescue numbers of people are built of reasons to rescue particular individuals. Because A and B are different particular individuals, there is a moral difference between saving A rather than A and C in *Costless No-Conflict* and saving A rather than B and C in *Costless Conflict*. In the former case, whether you save A only or save A and C, you respond to the reason to save A, and so saving A only allows C to die gratuitously. In the latter case, saving A does not allow C to die gratuitously since in that case letting C (and B) die is the only way to respond to the reason to save A.

What makes it wrong to save the lesser number in cases like *Costless Conflict* is simply that there is more requiring reason overall to save the greater number (B and C) and no sufficiently strong permitting reason to save the lesser number (A).

This explanation invites the following objection. If the requiring reasons to save B's life and C's life together outweigh the requiring reason to save A's life, then presumably the requiring reasons to save B's life and C's *finger* together outweigh the requiring reason to save A's life. But it's not wrong to save A's life instead of saving B's life and C's finger.

Of course, those who find it intuitively wrong to save A's life instead of saving B's life and C's finger will not be moved by this objection. They can accept my explanation of what makes it wrong to save the lesser number in cases like *Costless Conflict* as it stands. But it seems to me permissible to save A's life instead of saving *B*'s life and *C*'s finger. So I need to supplement my explanation.

(Some hold that you are required to toss a coin to determine whether to save *A*'s life or *B*'s life, thereby giving each a 50 percent chance of being saved.[3] Some likewise hold that you are required to toss a coin to determine whether to save *A*'s life or *B*'s life along with *C*'s finger. I am skeptical. At least in one-off rescue scenarios in which your choice does not involve invidious discrimination, it seems to me permissible to save either *A*'s life or *B*'s life without first tossing a coin, even when saving *B*'s life comes with the bonus of saving *C*'s finger. Rather than employing a randomizing procedure, it seems permissible to select arbitrarily—saving whomever is nearer, seen first, or to your left. Henceforth I suppose that there are no requiring reasons to randomize. Those who disagree can transpose the relevant arguments accordingly. But it is worth noting that it would still seem permissible to save *A*'s life instead of saving *B*'s life and *C*'s finger even if there were no randomizing procedure available.)

In what follows, I supplement my explanation of what makes it wrong to save the lesser number in cases like *Costless Conflict* so that it is compatible with the claim that it is permissible to save *A*'s life instead of saving *B*'s life and *C*'s finger.

The balance of requiring reasons is not what makes it permissible to save *A*'s life instead of saving *B*'s life and *C*'s finger. There is a strong requiring reason to save *A*'s life, an equally strong requiring reason to save *B*'s life, and a much weaker but still significant requiring reason to save *C*'s finger. It is accordingly plausible that there is more requiring reason overall to save *B*'s life along with *C*'s finger than there is to save *A*'s life.

Although it is plausible that there is more requiring reason overall to save *B*'s life along with *C*'s finger than there is to save *A*'s life, it still seems *permissible* to save *A*'s life instead of saving *B*'s life along with *C*'s finger. It is permissible to save *A*'s life when the alternative is saving *B*'s life, and it seems that adding *C*'s finger to "*B*'s side" of the conflict cannot by itself make it wrong to save *A*'s life. It cannot so easily be made wrong to save *A*'s life.

These claims support the view that there are permitting reasons to help particular individuals—what I call *individualist permitting reasons*. There is a strong requiring reason to save *A*'s life, but there is in addition a strong permitting reason to save *A*'s life (likewise for *B*, of course). The individualist permitting reason to save *A*'s life is strong enough to make it permissible to save *A*'s life, even though there is more requiring reason overall to save *B*'s life along with *C*'s finger. However, the individualist permitting reason to save *A*'s life is *not* strong enough to make it permissible to save *A*'s life in cases like *Costless Conflict*, in which you can instead save the lives of both *B* and *C*. This is because while there's *somewhat* more requiring reason overall to save *B*'s life and *C*'s finger than there is to save *A*'s life, there's *substantially* more requiring reason overall to save *B*'s life and *C*'s life than there is to save *A*'s life. While adding *C*'s finger to *B*'s side of the conflict cannot plausibly make it wrong to save *A*, adding *C*'s *life* can.

It may not be immediately obvious that there is *both* a requiring reason to save *A* *and* an individualist permitting reason to do so. But individualist permitting reasons earn their keep by explaining intuitive claims like that it is permissible to save *A*'s life instead of saving *B*'s life and *C*'s finger. They show how these intuitive claims can be accommodated alongside other intuitive claims, like that it is wrong to save A's life instead of saving B's life and C's life.

Crucially, an individualist permitting reason to help a particular individual, A, does not serve to make it permissible to do an alternative whenever A is helped in this alternative. Instead, it serves to make it permissible to do one alternative rather than another alternative when A is helped in the first alternative but not in the second (or is helped to a greater extent in the first alternative than in the second). In the no-conflict case in which you can either costlessly save A's life or costlessly save A's life along with C's finger, there is no individualist permitting reason to save A's life only rather than save A's life along with C's finger since A is (equally) helped in both alternatives. But in the conflict case in which you can either costlessly save A's life or costlessly save B's life along with C's finger, there is a strong individualist permitting reason to save A's life rather than save B's life along with C's finger. Individualist permitting reasons capture an important difference between no-conflict cases and conflict cases. Saving A is not morally equivalent to saving B in a way that would validate the inference from the claim that it is wrong to save A's life instead of saving A's life and C's finger (or life) to the claim that it is wrong to save A's life instead of saving B's life and C's finger (or life).

In sum, while there is more requiring reason overall to save B's life along with C's finger than there is to save A's life, there is a sufficiently strong individualist permitting reason to save A's life rather than save B's life and C's finger. So, it is permissible to save A's life. By contrast, in *Costless Conflict*, there is more requiring reason overall to save B's life and C's life than there is to save A's life and no sufficiently strong permitting reason to save *A*'s life. So, in *Costless Conflict* it is wrong to save *A*'s life.

2.3. Individualism versus Aggregationism

In *Costless Conflict* it is not only wrong to save the lesser number. It is required to save the greater number. There's most requiring reason overall to save the greater number and no sufficiently strong permitting reason not to. In this section, I consider and respond to the following counterargument.[4]

(1) You are not required to do act *A* unless there is some individual to whom you owe it that you do act *A*.

(2) There is no individual to whom you owe it that you save the greater number in cases like *Costless Conflict*.

So,

(3) You are not required to save the greater number in cases like *Costless Conflict*.

Those who accept (1) hold that what you are required to do is determined by what you owe to others, taken individually.[5] Suppose we line everyone up and proceed one by one, asking of each whether you owe it to that particular individual whether you do *A*. If the answer is "no" at each step down the line—so that there is no individual to whom you owe it that you do *A*—then you are not required to do *A*. Those who accept (2) argue that, since what each member of the larger group stands to lose is no greater than what each member of the smaller group stands to lose, you do not owe it to anyone *individually* that you save the greater number (some defenders of [2] hold that you owe it to each individually that you give them an equal chance of being saved by tossing a coin to determine which group to save).

We might respond to this argument by claiming that, while its premises are plausible, it is more implausible to accept its conclusion than it is to reject a premise. That is, accepting (3) is more implausible than rejecting (1) or (2).

But we need not be this concessive. For it is not clear that we even find (1) and (2) plausible if, with most others, we find (3) implausible. There are bold and modest interpretations of (1). On the bold interpretation, (1) says that what you are required to do is determined by what you owe to others taken individually in a way that precludes a requirement to save *two* strangers rather than *one* other stranger. But then those of us who find (3) implausible will find (1) (boldly interpreted) directly implausible. On the modest interpretation, (1) says that what you are required to do is determined by what you owe to others taken individually in a way that does *not* preclude a requirement to save two strangers rather than one other stranger. But then those of us who find (3) implausible and find (1) (modestly interpreted) plausible will find (2) directly implausible. We will then find it plausible that you owe it to each of the two strangers that you save them over the one.

We do not find (1) and (2) plausible, if we find (3) implausible. But even if we do not find (1) and (2) plausible, there could still be good independent reasons to accept their conjunction.

A possible independent reason to accept the conjunction of (1) and (2) is that it prohibits *interpersonal aggregation*, or "aggregation" for short. That is, it prohibits combining requiring reasons to help separate individuals so that there is more requiring reason overall to help a larger group than there is to help a smaller group (when there wouldn't be otherwise). But it seems requiring reasons can combine in this way. Intuitively, there is more requiring reason overall to prevent a million people from each suffering a year of agony than there is to prevent one other person from suffering a year of equally intense agony. And, intuitively, there is more requiring reason overall to save *B*'s life and *C*'s life than there is to save *A*'s life.

Absent an argument against aggregation, the fact that the conjunction of (1) and (2) prohibits aggregation would appear to be a reason to reject this conjunction, rather than accept it. For it appears we ought to be able to aggregate.

One worry is that aggregation overlooks the moral significance of the fact that different people are different.[6] But the previous section shows this worry to be unfounded. Aggregation does not imply that saving *A* rather than *B* and *C* is morally akin to saving *A* rather than *A* and *C*. The latter allows *C* to die gratuitously; the former does not. There are individualist permitting reasons to save the lesser number in conflict cases, but not in no-conflict cases.

Another worry is that aggregation will run amok. Suppose you can either save one person from very intense agony or save 10 others from slightly less intense agony. If the requiring reasons to save each of the 10 aggregate, it seems there would be more requiring reason overall to save the 10 than to save the one. Next suppose you can either save these 10 or save 100 others from slightly less intense agony still. Again, it seems there would be more requiring reason overall to save the 100 than to save the 10. After several such iterations, we appear to find ourselves with the counterintuitive conclusion that there is more requiring reason overall to save billions of people from very mild pain than there is to save one person from very intense agony.[7]

This problem does not give us reason to doubt that, when each face sufficiently similar harms, there is more requiring reason overall to save B and C than there is to save A. If we are not prepared to accept the counterintuitive "fully aggregative" conclusion above, we should instead opt for a "partially aggregative" view. According to the latter sort of view, when the harms in question are sufficiently similar, there can be more requiring reason overall to save a greater number of people each from lesser harm than there is to save a lesser number of people each from greater harm. We can then claim that while there is more requiring reason overall to save 10 people from intense agony than there is to save one from slightly more intense agony (these harms are sufficiently similar), there is more requiring reason overall to save one person from intense agony than there is to save any number from very mild pain (these harms are sufficiently different). Problems with full aggregation do not give us good independent reason to accept the conjunction of (1) and (2), thereby prohibiting any aggregation.[8]

The above argument appealing to (1) and (2) does not support the conclusion that you are not required to save the greater number in cases like *Costless Conflict*. If we find this argument's conclusion implausible, we will not find its premises plausible. And there appears to be no good independent reason to accept its premises.

2.4. Differences in Quality of Life

In section 2.2, I argued that while there's more requiring reason overall to save B's life along with C's finger than there is to save A's life, there's a sufficiently strong individualist permitting reason to save A's life instead of saving B's life and C's finger. So, in this case it is permissible to save A's life. But I argued that, in *Costless Conflict*, there's more requiring reason overall to save B's life and C's life than there is to save A's life and no sufficiently strong permitting reason to save A's life. So, in *Costless Conflict* it is wrong to save A's life. We might worry that this reasoning will have implausible implications in cases in which there are large differences in the remaining *quality of life* of those you can save. Consider the following case.[9]

> *Bored v. Joyful*: Two strangers, Bored and Joyful, face a deadly threat. You can do nothing, save Bored's life at no cost to yourself, or save Joyful's life at no cost to yourself. You cannot save both. So far each has lived a boring, somewhat empty life. If Bored is saved, their life will go on in this fashion. But if Joyful is saved, their life will change for much the better. If saved, each would live another 40 years. While Bored's remaining life would be decent, Joyful's would contain much more of what makes life worth living.

It seems plausible that, even though Joyful's remaining life would be much better than Bored's, you are not required to save Joyful's life. But we might worry that if the individualist permitting reason to save *A*'s life in *Costless Conflict* isn't strong enough to make it permissible to save *A*'s life given that there's substantially more requiring reason overall to save the lives of *B* and *C*, then the individualist permitting reason to save Bored's life in *Bored v. Joyful* won't be strong enough to make it permissible to save Bored's life if there's substantially more requiring reason overall to save Joyful's life.

I submit that those of us who find it plausible that it is permissible to save Bored's life will not find it plausible that there's substantially more requiring reason overall to save Joyful's life than there is to save Bored's. There's a strong requiring reason to prevent a stranger from losing out on a *decent* life, but intuitively there isn't a much stronger requiring reason to prevent a stranger from losing out on a much better life.[10] (This mirrors an intuitive asymmetry between preventing significant harms and providing pure benefits to those who are sufficiently well off.)

It is plausible that there isn't more requiring reason overall to save Joyful's life than there is to save Bored's life. But even if there is, it remains plausible that there isn't so much more requiring reason overall to save Joyful's life than there is to save Bored's life that the individualist permitting reason to save Bored's life isn't strong enough to make it permissible to save Bored's life. So, it is permissible to save Bored's life in *Bored v. Joyful*. But in *Costless Conflict* there *is* so much more requiring reason overall to save the lives of *B* and *C* than there is to save *A*'s life that the individualist permitting reason to save *A*'s life isn't strong enough to make it permissible to save *A*'s life. So, it is wrong to save *A*'s life in *Costless Conflict*.[11]

2.5. Scaling Up the Numbers

In *Costless Conflict*, there's more requiring reason overall to save *B*'s life and *C*'s life than there is to save *A*'s life and no sufficiently strong permitting reason to save *A*'s life. So, in *Costless Conflict* it is wrong to save *A*'s life.

What should we say when you can either save the lives of 100 strangers or instead save the lives of 101 different strangers? The requiring reasons to save each are equally strong. It is accordingly plausible that there is more requiring reason overall to save the 101 than there is to save the 100 others. So, whether it is permissible to save the 100 depends on whether there is a sufficiently strong permitting reason to do so. If the permitting reason to save the 100 were no stronger than the individualist permitting reason to save one person (i.e., no stronger than the individualist permitting reason to save *A* in *Costless Conflict*), then it would be wrong to save the 100 instead of the 101 others. However, it is plausible that the individualist permitting reasons to save each of the 100 *together* constitute a sufficiently strong permitting reason to save the 100 instead of the 101. It is plausible that it is permissible to save the 100, even though there's more requiring reason overall to save the 101.[12] But when you can either save the lives of 100 strangers or instead save the lives of *200* different strangers, the individualist permitting reasons to save each of the 100 do not together make it permissible to save the 100. In general, you are required to save the lives of 2*N* strangers instead of saving the lives of *N* different strangers. (In *Costless Conflict*, *N* = 1.)

There is a potential complication. Some might hold that, when each of two available alternatives provides enough help, there is a (sufficiently strong) *satisficing* permitting reason to do either, even if there is more requiring reason overall to do one alternative than there is to do the other.[13] For example, they might hold that, even though you are required to save B's finger and C's finger rather than save A's finger, you are—thanks to satisficing permitting reasons—permitted to save the lives of 100 strangers and A's finger rather than save the lives of these same 100 strangers, B's finger, and C's finger. I do not here take a stand on whether this is correct. But even if it is, satisficing permitting reasons would seem to have their limits. First, when two alternatives are perfectly alike but for the fact that one allows additional significant harm (i.e., it allows this extra harm *gratuitously*), it seems there cannot be a sufficiently strong satisficing permitting reason to do the former, no matter how much help it provides.[14] For example, you are required to save the lives of 100 strangers and A's finger rather than save the lives of these same 100 strangers. Second, when two alternatives are perfectly alike but for the fact that one includes allowing $2N$ strangers to die, whereas the other includes allowing N different strangers to die, it seems there cannot be a sufficiently strong satisficing permitting reason to do the former, no matter how much help it provides. For example, you are required to save the lives of 100 strangers and save B's life and C's life rather than save the lives of these same 100 strangers and save A's life.

2.6. An Analogy with Doing Harm

Although the claim that you are required to save the greater number in cases like *Costless Conflict* seems adequately defended already, there is a further argument in its defense.[15] Consider the following case.

> *Harmful Conflict*: You face a severe harm. You can do nothing, save yourself in a way that moderately harms one stranger, or save yourself in another way that equally harms each of two other strangers.

Suppose, for the sake of concrete illustration, that a boulder is hurtling toward you. If you do nothing, you will be crushed to death. You can save yourself by effortlessly kicking a log to your left. This will cause the boulder to roll to the left, which has the foreseeable side effect of crushing the foot of one stranger. You can instead save yourself by effortlessly kicking a log to your right. This will cause the boulder to roll to the right, which has the foreseeable side effect of crushing two feet, each belonging to one of two other strangers.

Assuming there is a big enough gap between "severe" harm and "moderate" harm, there is a sufficiently strong permitting reason to save yourself in *Harmful Conflict*. But it is wrong to save yourself in a way that harms the two strangers (it would be permissible were it the only way to save yourself). In cases like *Harmful Conflict*, there is more requiring reason overall not to harm B and C than there is not to harm A and no sufficiently strong individualist permitting reason to harm B and C rather than A. Next consider the following argument.

(1) If, when the harms for each are sufficiently similar, there is more requiring reason overall not to harm B and C

than there is not to harm *A* (and no sufficiently strong individualist permitting reason to harm *B* and *C* rather than *A*), then, when the harms for each are sufficiently similar, there is more requiring reason overall *to save B and C* than there is *to save A* (and no sufficiently strong individualist permitting reason to save *A* rather than *B* and *C*).

(2) When the harms for each are sufficiently similar, there is more requiring reason overall not to harm *B* and *C* than there is not to harm *A* (and no sufficiently strong individualist permitting reason to harm *B* and *C* rather than *A*).

So,

(3) When the harms for each are sufficiently similar, there is more requiring reason overall to save *B* and *C* than there is to save *A* (and no sufficiently strong individualist permitting reason to save *A* rather than *B* and *C*).

It is plausible that requiring reasons not to do harm to others are stronger than requiring reasons not to allow harm to others (i.e., requiring reasons to save others from harm).[16] The idea behind (1) is that, even if doing harm and allowing harm are different, they are not *radically* different, and so neither are the reasons to avoid them. If conflicting reasons to avoid doing harm at least partially aggregate, then conflicting reasons to avoid allowing harm at least partially aggregate. And plausible claims about cases like *Harmful Conflict* imply that conflicting reasons to avoid doing harm at least partially aggregate. If successful, this argument provides further support for the claim that, in cases like *Costless Conflict*, you are required to save the greater number.

Notes

1. There may for all that be *non-requiring* reasons to give out candy. Such reasons may be neither requiring nor permitting but merely "commendatory." See Little and Macnamara 2017. Also see Horgan and Timmons 2010 on "merit-conferring" reasons and Dancy 2004 on "enticing" reasons.

2. See Glover 1977 (207–209) and Kavka 1979 (291–292). For a similar argument for the different conclusion that it is *better* to save *B* and *C* than to save *A*, see Kamm 1993 and Hirose 2014.

3. On deciding by lot, see Broome 1990, Kamm 1993, Timmermann 2004, Bradley 2009, and Walden 2014.

4. See Anscombe 1967, Taurek 1977, and Munoz-Dardé 2005.

5. Some accept (1) but reject (2) and (3). For discussion, see Kamm 1993, Scanlon 1998 (232), Wasserman and Strudler 2003, Otsuka 2006, and Kumar 2011.

6. On the moral importance of the separateness of persons, see Rawls 1971 (27), Nozick 1974 (32–33), Liao 2008, and Brink 2020.

7. See Rachels 1998, Temkin 2012, and Pummer 2018. In response to this sort of argument, we can reject a step, accept the conclusion, or reject the transitivity of "more requiring reason overall than" (i.e., reject the claim that, if there is more requiring reason overall to do *A* than there is to do *B* and there is more requiring reason overall to do *B* than there is to do *C*, then there is more requiring reason overall to do *A* than there is to do *C*, when *A*, *B*, and *C* are members of the same set of alternatives).

8. For further discussion of full versus partial aggregation, see Parfit 2003, Kamm 2007, Voorhoeve 2014, and Horton 2021. Note that, even if we reject full aggregation, we could still allow that there is some number of headaches each for a separate person such that you are required to save

B's life while preventing this many headaches instead of saving *A*'s life (in other words, even if no number of headaches can outweigh a life, perhaps some number of headaches *and a life* can together outweigh another life). Whether this is so would depend on the strength of the individualist permitting reason to save *A*'s life—it's plausibly strong enough to make it permissible to save *A*'s life instead of saving *B*'s life while preventing *several* headaches, but it's not clear that this permitting reason is strong enough to make it permissible to save *A*'s life instead of saving *B*'s life while preventing *any* number of headaches.

9. From Doggett 2013.

10. Were Bored's remaining life not decent, there would be more requiring reason overall to save Joyful. I do not here take a stand on what counts as "decent" (in terms of quality or length of life). But notice that even if the bar were set quite high, there could nonetheless be an enormous disparity between Bored's barely decent remaining life and Joyful's *extraordinarily* good remaining life. For relevant discussion, see debates about allocating scarce life-saving resources on the basis of maximizing quality-adjusted life-years. For example, Singer et al. 1995, Harris 1995, Kamm 2009, and Chappell 2016.

11. Doggett 2013 argues that, if you are not required to save Joyful's life along with *C*'s finger rather than save Bored's life, then you are not required to save the lives of *B* and *C* rather than save *A*'s life. He argues that these cases are relevantly analogous (e.g., in both cases, saving the greater number has a much better outcome). The view I've offered here provides a crucial disanalogy between the cases: while there is a strong requiring reason to save someone's life (if it's at least decent), there is a relatively weak requiring reason to save someone's finger. There is more requiring reason overall to save Joyful's life along with *C*'s finger than there is to save Bored's life but not so much more that the individualist permitting reason to save Bored's life cannot make it permissible to save Bored's life.

12. By contrast, according to Kamm's 2007 (58) method of balancing, the 100 people on one side "silence" 100 of those on the other side and leave one unsilenced so that you are required to save the 101 instead of the 100 others. Those who find it plausible that you are required to save the 101

could hold that the individualist permitting reasons to save each of the 100 do not aggregate in the way needed for them to together make it permissible to save the 100 instead of the 101.

13. Views according to which there are satisficing permitting reasons are not to be confused with views of satisficing according to which, when each of two available alternatives provides enough help, there's no more requiring reason overall to do one than there is to do the other, even if one provides (much) more help than the other. Also notice that what counts as "enough" help can be understood as an absolute amount of help or as a percentage of the most help you can provide at a given time. See Hurka 1990 and Mulgan 1993 for discussions of Slote's 1985 view of satisficing.

14. I take it that even if two alternatives save the same number of people, they can fail to be perfectly alike if they involve saving *different* people.

15. This argument is inspired by Kamm 2005 (2) and Woollard 2014.

16. See, for example, Woollard 2015. For arguments against the moral relevance of the distinction between doing and allowing, see Kagan 1989.

3 | THE ALL OR NOTHING PROBLEM

3.1. When It's Wrong to Save One Yet Okay to Save None

In Chapter 1, I claimed that you are not required to save the life of a stranger when the cost to you is great, even if it is much less than death (*Costly Rescue*). For example, you are not required to put your legs in the path of a boulder to prevent it from crushing a stranger to death. Even if this were the only way to save the lives of two strangers, you could permissibly refrain from incurring such a great cost. While there are requiring reasons to save lives, great costs can yield sufficiently strong permitting reasons not to save lives.

In Chapter 2, I claimed that it is wrong to save one stranger's life at no cost to yourself when you can instead save both this stranger's life *and* another's at no cost to yourself (*Costless No-Conflict*). There is most requiring reason overall to save both lives and no sufficiently strong permitting reason not to do so. I also claimed that it is wrong to save one stranger's life at no cost to yourself when you can instead save the lives of two other strangers

The Rules of Rescue. Theron Pummer, Oxford University Press. © Oxford University Press 2023.
DOI: 10.1093/oso/9780190884147.003.0004

at no cost to yourself (*Costless Conflict*). There is most requiring reason overall to save the two and no sufficiently strong permitting reason not to do so.

In this chapter, I consider a problem that arises in cases like the following.[1]

> *Costly No-Conflict*: Two strangers face a deadly threat. You can do nothing, save one stranger's life at great cost to yourself, or save both their lives at the same great cost to yourself.

> *Costly Conflict*: Three strangers face a deadly threat. You can do nothing, save one stranger's life at great cost to yourself, or save the other two at the same great cost to yourself.

In the first instance, I explore the problem in the context of *Costly No-Conflict*. For a concrete illustration of this case, suppose that a boulder to your left is hurtling toward one stranger and that a boulder to your right is hurtling toward another stranger. If you do nothing, both strangers will be crushed to death. You can save one stranger by putting your legs in the path of the left boulder. You can instead save both strangers by putting your legs in the path of the right boulder—this will deflect the right boulder in a way that also deflects the left boulder.

In *Costly No-Conflict*, there is most requiring reason overall to save both lives yet also a sufficiently strong permitting reason to do nothing. Accordingly, it is permissible to save both lives, and it is permissible to do nothing. But is it permissible to save one stranger's life at great cost to yourself when you can instead save both this stranger's life *and* another's at the same cost to yourself?

Intuitively, it is not.[2] Moreover, there is a natural explanation of why it is wrong to save the lesser number in *Costly No-Conflict*.

First, there is more requiring reason overall to save the greater number than there is to save the lesser number. This would make it wrong to save the lesser number, if there were no sufficiently strong permitting reason to do so.

And, second, there is no such permitting reason. While there is a strong cost-based permitting reason not to save the lesser number (and not to save the greater number), there is no cost-based permitting reason *to* save the lesser number. For this, there would have to be some alternative that is costlier to you than saving the lesser number so that saving the lesser number avoids this cost. But the only alternatives are doing nothing and saving the greater number, and neither is costlier to you than saving the lesser number. Moreover, there is no sufficiently strong autonomy-based permitting reason to save the lesser number.[3] Apart from determining whether a stranger lives or dies, your choice between saving the lesser number and saving the greater number does not make a significant difference to how your life unfolds. Given this, it is not plausible that there is a significant autonomy-based permitting reason to save the lesser number. Similarly, when the only significant difference between costlessly using what is yours in one way and costlessly using what is yours in another way is whether a stranger lives or dies, there is no significant autonomy-based permitting reason to use what is yours in the way that allows the stranger to die.

In sum, in *Costly No-Conflict*, there is more requiring reason overall to save the greater number than there is to do either alternative. But while there is a sufficiently strong permitting reason to do nothing, there is no sufficiently strong permitting reason to save the lesser number. It is permissible to save both strangers, permissible to do nothing, and wrong to save just one stranger. In the remainder of this chapter, I discuss a potential problem involving this combination of claims. After presenting the problem (section 3.2), I present four possible solutions (sections 3.3, 3.4, 3.5, and 3.6) and reject all but the last one. I then show how my solution can be similarly applied to conflict cases (section 3.7).

3.2. The Problem

Consider the following argument.

(1) In *Costly No-Conflict*, it is permissible to save both strangers, and it is permissible to do nothing.
(2) In *Costly No-Conflict*, it is wrong to save just one stranger.
(3) When *A* and *B* are your only permissible alternatives, if you are not going to do *B*, you are required to do *A*.

So,

(4) In *Costly No-Conflict*, if you are not going to save both strangers, you are required to do nothing.

For the reasons offered in section 3.1, we should accept claims (1) and (2). But, together with the seemingly plausible claim (3), they imply the seemingly implausible conclusion (4). This is known as the *all or nothing problem*.[4]

The all or nothing problem concerns *conditional requirements*.[5] Conditional requirements provide guidance for agents who are not going to perform certain acts that are available to them, including when they are not going to do what they are required to do. For example, you are required not to commit murder, whether you do it brutally or gently; but there is a sense in which *if* you are going to murder, you are required to murder gently.

There is an immediate question about how to understand conditional-requirement claims. These claims appear to have the form "if P, then Q." Logic tells us that from "if P, then Q" and "P" it follows that "Q." For instance, from "if you are a human, then you are a mammal" and "you are a human," it follows that "you are a mammal." Similarly, it would appear that from "if you are going to murder, then you are required to murder gently" and "you are going to murder," it follows that "you are required to murder gently." Of course, you are not required to murder gently. You are required to refrain from murdering altogether. So conditional-requirement claims like "if you are going to murder, then you are required to murder gently" must be understood in a way that prohibits the derivation of a "plain old" non-conditional requirement to murder gently from the fact that you are going to murder. I take it that claims like "if you are going to murder, then you are required to murder gently" are more plausibly understood as claims like "you are required to (murder gently, given that you are going to murder)." It does not follow from "you are required to (murder gently, given that you are going to murder)" and "you are going to murder" that "you are required to murder gently."[6] Morality gives us the guidance not to murder, but it also gives us the guidance to murder gently *given that* we are going to murder.

It is important to keep the above issue about how to understand conditional-requirement claims in mind when considering (3) and (4). For example, I understand (4) as the claim that "you are required to (do nothing, given that you are not going to save both strangers)." It does not follow from (4) so understood, together with the fact that you are not going to save both strangers, that you are plain old non-conditionally required to do nothing. Even so, (4) seems to offer bad guidance. It is implausible that morality would guide you to let the one stranger die given that you are not going to save both.

The all or nothing problem is a problem to the extent that the premises (1), (2), and (3) are plausible, while the conclusion (4) is implausible. In the next four sections, I discuss four possible solutions, which correspond to rejecting each of the premises and to accepting the conclusion. I argue that we should reject (3). However, it is worth remembering that readers who favor different solutions can feel free to transpose my arguments from the point of departure, seeing where they lead. For example, those who accept (4) could still accept a set of claims that is very similar to what I defend over the course of the book.

3.3. Okay to Go Beyond What Is Okay

According to (2), in *Costly No-Conflict*, it is wrong to save just one stranger. Here is an argument for rejecting (2). First, if act *A* is permissible and there is more requiring reason overall to do *B* than there is to do *A*, then *B* is permissible.[7] Second, in *Costly*

THE ALL OR NOTHING PROBLEM 67

No-Conflict, it is permissible to do nothing, and there is more requiring reason overall to save just one stranger than there is to do nothing. Therefore, in *Costly No-Conflict*, it is permissible to save just one stranger.

This proposed solution to the all or nothing problem fails. Were the permissibility of acts determined solely by the balance of requiring reasons, it would seem to follow that if act *A* is permissible and there is more requiring reason overall to do *B* than there is to do *A*, then *B* is permissible. If act *B* has more of the property that makes acts permissible than an act *A* that is itself permissible, then *B* is permissible too.

However, the permissibility of acts is determined by the balance of requiring reasons *and* permitting reasons. In *Costly No-Conflict*, there is least requiring reason overall to do nothing, more requiring reason overall to save just one stranger, and most requiring reason overall to save both strangers. It is permissible to do nothing because there is a sufficiently strong permitting reason to do so. It is wrong to save just one stranger because there is more requiring reason overall to save both strangers and no sufficiently strong permitting reason to save just one. In this case, there is more requiring reason overall to do an act that is wrong than there is to do an act that is permissible.[8]

3.4. Reasons to Avoid Doing What Is Wrong

According to (4), in *Costly No-Conflict*, if you are not going to save both strangers, you are required to do nothing. As I mentioned, there is a question about how to understand such conditional claims: (4) would be unproblematic if it were saying nothing more than that *to act permissibly*, you must do nothing given that you are not going to save both. It would then collapse into a report of the non-conditional permissibility of your alternatives.[9] Instead, I understand (4) as the claim that, "you are required to (do nothing, given that you are not going to save both strangers)." So understood, (4) is not a report of the non-conditional permissibility of your alternatives. Instead, it is guidance to let the one stranger die given that you are not going to save both. But this seems like bad guidance. Thus, (4) is implausible.

Nonetheless, according to some philosophers, there is a decisive requiring reason not to perform an act that is wrong, so that there is always more requiring reason overall to perform an act that is permissible than there is to perform an act that is wrong.[10] They might argue that, since it is wrong to save just one stranger, there is more requiring reason overall to do nothing than there is to save just one stranger. And if there is more requiring reason overall to do nothing than there is to save just one stranger, then it does not seem implausible that you are required to (do nothing, given that you are not going to save both strangers). Philosophers who hold that there is a decisive reason not to perform an act that is wrong can in this way defend (4). Does this proposed solution to the all or nothing problem succeed?

If all that makes it wrong to save just one stranger is that there is more requiring reason overall to save both and no sufficiently strong permitting reason to save just one rather than save both, then it does not seem plausible that the fact that it is wrong to save just one is a requiring reason to do nothing rather than save just one. Even if this fact were *a* requiring reason to do nothing rather than save just one, it would not plausibly make it the case that there is more requiring reason overall to do nothing than there is to save just one.[11] So, the above defense of (4) fails.

However, some claim that it is not merely that there is more requiring reason overall to save both and no sufficiently strong permitting reason to save just one that makes it wrong to save just one. They claim that there is (also) a requiring reason not to perform an act that allows a stranger to die *gratuitously*. After all, saving just one stranger in *Costly No-Conflict* disregards the other stranger, treating them as if they count for nothing.[12]

It is plausible that there is a requiring reason not to perform an act that allows a stranger to die gratuitously. Suppose you can do nothing, prevent one stranger from stubbing their toe (at great cost to yourself), or prevent this stranger from stubbing their toe *and* save another stranger's life (at the same great cost to yourself). Arguably, a requiring reason not to perform an act that allows a stranger to die gratuitously makes it the case that there is more requiring reason overall to do nothing than there is to prevent the stranger from stubbing their toe without saving the other stranger's life. Arguably, you are required to (help neither, given that you're not going to help both). But it is not plausible that a requiring reason not to perform an act that allows a stranger to die gratuitously makes it the case that, in *Costly No-Conflict*, there is more requiring reason overall to do nothing than there is to save just one.[13] So, again, the above defense of (4) fails.

3.5. Willingness and Motivation

According to (1), in *Costly No-Conflict*, it is permissible to save both strangers, and it is permissible to do nothing. Act consequentialists reject (1). They claim that, since you're required to bring about the best outcome, you're required to save both strangers in *Costly No-Conflict*. Act consequentialism is implausible for its failure to recognize moral permissions (among other things). But there is a way to reject (1) without rejecting moral permissions altogether. Some have argued that facts about your willingness or motivation in *Costly No-Conflict* can make it the case that it is wrong to do nothing.

According to a *willingness*-based solution, if in *Costly No-Conflict* you are willing to incur the great cost of saving at least one of the strangers, there is no sufficiently strong permitting reason to do nothing (since when you are willing to incur the cost of helping others, this cost does not provide a permitting reason not to help).[14] Since then there's most requiring reason overall to save both and no sufficiently strong permitting reason not to, you are required to save both. When you are willing to incur the great cost of saving at least one of the strangers, it is—contrary to (1)— wrong to do nothing.[15]

According to a *motivation*-based solution, if in *Costly No-Conflict* your motivation for doing nothing isn't to avoid the cost of helping, there is no sufficiently strong permitting reason to do nothing (since when your motivation for not helping isn't to avoid the cost of helping, this cost does not provide a permitting reason not to help).[16] To illustrate, suppose that in *Costly No-Conflict* you are just as averse to losing your legs as the next person, but you are unusually moved by the plight of stranger *A*. Were your only alternatives to either do nothing or save *A* at the cost of your legs, you would save *A*. But in *Costly No-Conflict*, you can do nothing, save *A* at the cost of your legs, or save *A* and *B* at the cost of your legs. You unjustifiably hate *B* and are strongly moved not to save *B*. Since you are also strongly moved to avoid criticism for saving just *A* when you could have also saved *B* at no extra cost, you save neither. Your motivation for not helping others is not to avoid incurring the cost of doing so (while you are moved to a significant extent to avoid the loss of your legs, this isn't your motivating reason to refrain from helping). Therefore, according to the motivation-based solution, the cost of your legs does not provide a permitting reason not to help. When in *Costly No-Conflict* your motivation for not helping is not to avoid the cost of helping but unjustifiable hate for *B* (along with a desire to avoid criticism for saving just *A* when you could have also saved *B* at no extra cost), this solution implies that you are required to save both strangers at the cost of your legs—contrary to (1).

It is implausible to reject (1) in the ways implied by the willingness-based solution and the motivation-based solution. First, it seems that even if facts about willingness or motivation prevented costs from providing permitting reasons, there could still be sufficiently strong autonomy-based permitting reasons not to help. Even if you couldn't appeal to the fact that losing your legs is costly, presumably you could still appeal to the fact that whether you keep your legs makes a significant difference to how your life unfolds.

Second, it seems that neither willingness nor motivation prevents costs from providing permitting reasons in the ways implied by these solutions. Even when you are willing to incur the great cost of helping others, or when your motivation for not helping isn't to avoid incurring the great cost of doing so, the great cost of helping can still make it permissible not to. This seems to me true in *Costly No-Conflict*. In addition, consider the following.

> *Your Life v. Stranger's Legs*: You can do nothing; press a red button, thereby saving stranger *A*'s legs; or press a green button, thereby saving stranger *A*'s legs and stranger *B*'s finger. Pressing either button will also cause you to drop into a fiery pit and die.

Suppose that in *Your Life v. Stranger's Legs* you are just as averse to dying a fiery death as the next person, but you are unusually moved by the plight of stranger *A*. To save *A*'s legs, you are willing to incur the cost of a fiery death (were your only alternatives to either do nothing or press the red button, you would press it). However, you unjustifiably hate stranger *B* and are strongly moved not to save their finger. Since you are also strongly moved to avoid criticism for pressing the red button, you do nothing. Your motivation for not helping others is not to avoid incurring the cost of doing so.

When these are the facts about willingness and motivation, the willingness-based solution and the motivation-based solution each imply that the enormous cost of dying a fiery death does not provide a permitting reason not to help, and so you are required to press the green button, saving *A*'s legs and *B*'s finger at this enormous cost to yourself. While you may be blameworthy for doing nothing out of such a bad motivation, it still seems permissible to do nothing (I return to blameworthiness in the next chapter). It seems implausible that you would be *required* to press the green button.

If there were no independently plausible solution to the all or nothing problem, it could be argued that, though the willingness-based solution and the motivation-based solution have implausible implications, one or the other way of rejecting (1) is the *least implausible* solution. But, as I argue in the following section, there is an independently plausible solution—it both is principled and has plausible implications in particular cases. So, this argument for rejecting (1) fails.

3.6. Conditional Permissibility

I understand (3) as the claim that, when A and B are your only permissible alternatives, you are required to (do A, given that you are not going to do B). In cases like the following, (3) has plausible implications.

> *Costless v. Costly*: Two strangers face a deadly threat. You can do nothing, save one stranger's life at no cost to yourself, or save both their lives at great cost to yourself.

In *Costless v. Costly*, it is wrong to do nothing, permissible to save just one stranger, and permissible to save both strangers (while there is a sufficiently strong permitting reason to do nothing rather than save both, there is no sufficiently strong permitting reason to do nothing rather than save just one; meanwhile, there is a sufficiently strong permitting reason to save just one rather than save both). Since saving just one stranger and saving both strangers are your only permissible alternatives, (3) has the implication that you are required to (save just one stranger, given that you are not going to save both strangers). This is plausible.

But in *Costly No-Conflict*, it is permissible to do nothing, wrong to save just one stranger, and permissible to save both strangers—at least according to (1) and (2). Since doing nothing and saving both strangers are your only permissible alternatives, (3) has the implication that you are required to (do nothing, given that you are not going to save both strangers). This is implausible. Morality would not steer you away from saving just one stranger given that you are not going to save both.

The correct solution to the all or nothing problem is to reject (3). In conditional-requirement claims like "you are required to (do *A*, given that you are not going to do *B*)," *B* is an *excluded alternative*. The problem with (3) is that it is prone to offer bad guidance for choosing among *non-excluded alternatives*; (3) offers bad guidance when it implies a conditional requirement to do a non-excluded alternative *A*, even though there is more requiring reason overall to do non-excluded alternative *C* than there is to do *A*. In *Costly No-Conflict*, (3) implies that you are required to (do nothing, given that you are not going to save both strangers). It implies this conditional requirement to do nothing even though there is more requiring reason overall to save just one stranger than there is to do nothing. Given that there can be more requiring reason overall to do a wrong act than to do a permissible act (as argued in section 3.4), (3) is implausible.

According to (3), non-conditional permissibility determines conditional permissibility. We should instead hold the view that *what determines* non-conditional permissibility also determines conditional permissibility. That is, just as the balance of requiring reasons and permitting reasons among your alternatives determines what is permissible, the balance of requiring reasons and permitting reasons among your *non-excluded* alternatives determines what is *conditionally* permissible.

Here is my view more fully. To determine whether a non-excluded act *A* is conditionally permissible, check whether there are any non-excluded alternatives to *A* that there is more requiring reason overall to do than there is to do *A*. If there are no non-excluded alternatives that there is more requiring reason overall to do than there is to do *A*, then *A* is conditionally permissible. If there are some non-excluded alternatives that there is more requiring reason overall to do than there is to do *A*, then, for each such non-excluded alternative *B*, check whether there is a sufficiently strong permitting reason to do *A* rather than *B*. If, for each such alternative *B*, there is a sufficiently strong permitting reason to do *A* rather than *B*, then *A* is conditionally permissible. Otherwise, *A* is conditionally wrong.[17]

(According to this view, the balance of requiring reasons and permitting reasons among your non-excluded alternatives determines what is conditionally permissible. But the view allows that excluded alternatives can affect the balance of requiring reasons and permitting reasons among non-excluded alternatives. Suppose that there is a requiring reason not to perform an act that allows a stranger to die gratuitously, so that in *Costly No-Conflict* there is a requiring reason against saving just one stranger. Even when saving both is an excluded alternative, the fact that it is an *alternative* makes it the case that saving just one allows someone to die gratuitously so that there is a requiring reason against saving just one stranger. However, as noted above, it is not plausible that a requiring reason not to perform an act that allows a stranger to die gratuitously outweighs the requiring reason to prevent the other stranger from dying. In *Costly No-Conflict*, there remains more requiring reason *overall* to save just one than there is to do nothing.[18])

This is a principled general view to take, and it has plausible implications in particular cases.

In *Costless v. Costly*, this view correctly implies that you are required to (save just one stranger, given that you are not going to save both strangers). There is more requiring reason overall to save just one than there is to do nothing, and no sufficiently strong permitting reason to do nothing rather than save just one.

In *Costly No-Conflict*, this view correctly implies that it is permissible to (save just one stranger, given that you are not going to save both) and permissible to (do nothing, given that you are not going to save both). There is more requiring reason overall to save just one than there is to do nothing and there is a sufficiently strong permitting reason to do nothing rather than save just one.

For the avoidance of doubt, the crucial point is not that in *Costly No-Conflict* there is more requiring reason overall to save just one than there is to do a *permissible* alternative (do nothing) but that, of your non-excluded alternatives (save just one and do nothing) there's no alternative A such that there is (i) more requiring reason overall to do A than there is to save just one and (ii) no sufficiently strong permitting reason to save just one rather than do *A*. Suppose your *four* alternatives are to do nothing, save one stranger at great cost, save this stranger and a second stranger at the same great cost, or save both these strangers and a third at the same great cost. Then the view proposed here correctly implies that, it is permissible to (save just two strangers, given that you are not going to save all three strangers) but wrong to (save just one stranger, given that you are not going to save all three strangers). There is more requiring reason overall to save just two than there is either to save just one or do nothing and there is no sufficiently strong permitting reason to save just one rather than save just two. The fact that there is more requiring reason overall to save just one than there is to do a permissible alternative (do nothing) does not imply that it is conditionally permissible to save just one.[19]

3.7. Conflict Cases

In Chapter 2, I claimed that it is wrong to save one stranger's life at no cost to yourself when you can instead save both this stranger's life and another's at no cost to yourself (*Costless No-Conflict*). There is most requiring reason overall to save both and no sufficiently strong permitting reason not to do so. In that chapter I also claimed that it is wrong to save one stranger's life at no cost to yourself when you can instead save the lives of two other strangers at no cost to yourself (*Costless Conflict*). There is most requiring reason overall to save the two and no sufficiently strong permitting reason not to do so.

In this chapter, I claimed that it is wrong to save one stranger's life at great cost to yourself when you can instead save both this stranger's life and another's at the same great cost to yourself (*Costly No-Conflict*). There is most requiring reason overall to save both, a sufficiently strong permitting reason to save neither, and no sufficiently strong permitting reason to save just one. We can next turn to a version of this case in which there is a conflict between the requiring reasons to rescue strangers.

> *Costly Conflict*: Three strangers face a deadly threat. You can do nothing, save one stranger's life at great cost to yourself, or save the other two at the same great cost to yourself.

In this case, there is most requiring reason overall to save the greater number, a sufficiently strong permitting reason to save no one, and no sufficiently strong permitting reason to save the lesser number. *Costly Conflict* is in this way like *Costly No-Conflict*. However, there are important differences between these cases.

In *Costly Conflict*, the requiring reasons to save the two strangers conflict with the requiring reason to save the one, whereas in *Costly No-Conflict* the requiring reasons to save both strangers do not conflict with the requiring reason to save just one. Recall from section 3.4 that some hold the view that, in *Costly No-Conflict*, not only is there more requiring reason overall to save both strangers than there is to save just one and no sufficiently strong permitting reason to save just one, but there is also a requiring reason not to perform an act that allows a stranger to die gratuitously. If this view is correct, then there is a reason against saving the lesser number in *Costly No-Conflict* that is absent in *Costly Conflict* as saving the lesser number in the latter does not allow anyone to die gratuitously. On this view, there is accordingly more to be said for the claim that you are required to (do nothing, given that you are not going to save the greater number) in *Costly No-Conflict* than in *Costly Conflict*.

Here is another important difference. While you are significantly praiseworthy for saving the greater number at great cost to yourself in both *Costly No-Conflict* and *Costly Conflict*, these cases differ with respect to the praiseworthiness of saving the lesser number at great cost to yourself. It is plausible that you can be significantly praiseworthy for saving the lesser number in *Costly Conflict*, even though this act is wrong. But you may not be praiseworthy overall for saving the lesser number in *Costly No-Conflict*. I discuss this difference in the next chapter.

One main claim of this book is that it can be wrong to save the lesser number even when it is permissible to save no one. This is so not only in cases like *Costly No-Conflict* and *Costly Conflict*, but in many other cases too. The claim that it is wrong to save the lesser number yet permissible to save no one gives rise to the all or nothing problem. How can we accept this claim while avoiding the implausible implication that you are required to (save no one, given that you are not going to save the greater number)? In this chapter, I considered several possible solutions to this problem, rejecting all but one. As argued in section 3.6, the correct solution is to adopt a view of conditional permissibility according to which, even when it is plain old wrong to save the lesser number, it can be permissible to (save the lesser number, given that you are not going to save the greater number). We can safely retain the claim that, in a variety of cases, it is wrong to save the lesser number even when it is permissible to save no one.

Notes

1. For similar cases, see Fried and Parfit 1979, Parfit 1982 (131), Pummer 2016a, Horton 2017a, Rulli 2020, and Muñoz 2021.

2. There is some evidence suggesting that most people share this intuition. See Caviola and Schubert unpublished.

3. See Chapter 1 on cost-based permitting reasons versus autonomy-based permitting reasons. Recall that autonomy-based permitting reasons are permitting reasons to determine your own life without contravening the rights of others.

4. For discussion, see Horton 2017a, McMahan 2018, Pummer 2019, Bader 2019, Muñoz 2021, Muñoz and Pummer 2022, Barry and Lazar 2022, Gordon-Solmon unpublished, and Tucker unpublished.

5. These are more commonly called "conditional obligations" or "conditional oughts." See Chisholm 1963, Forrester 1984, Jackson 1985, and McNamara 2019. Note that Horton 2017a (96) formulates (3) as a contrastive requirement (to do one act *rather than* another) but elsewhere (94) implies that it is equivalent to the conditional-requirement claim above.

6. Conditional-requirement claims in natural language appear to be narrow-scope conditional requirements, "if you do X, then you are required to do Y." But the case of gentle murder shows that this interpretation must be rejected when the consequent "you are required to do Y" cannot plausibly detach from the conditional given the antecedent "you do X." The wide-scope interpretation "you are required to see to it that (if you do X, then you do Y)" and the dyadic interpretation "you are required to (do Y, given that you do X)" each prohibit such detachment. See note 9 for why I favor the dyadic interpretation over the wide-scope interpretation. Alternatively, we could stick with narrow-scope conditional requirements, allowing for detachment of only suitably qualified consequents, e.g., "*in that case*, you are required to do Y." For further discussion, see Hansson 1969, Kratzer 2012, Silk 2014, Comesaña 2015, and Muñoz and Pummer 2022.

7. See Ferguson and Köhler 2020.

8. See Muñoz 2021.

9. I suspect the wide-scope interpretation of (4), "you are required to see to it that (if you are not going to save both strangers, then do nothing)," may be saying nothing more than that it is wrong to save just one stranger and permissible to do nothing. After all, this interpretation of (4) is equivalent to the disjunctive requirement "you are required to see to it that (you save both strangers or do nothing)," which looks like another way of saying that these are your only permissible alternatives. The dyadic interpretation of (4), "you are required to (do nothing, given that you are not going to save both strangers)," does not merely report that it is wrong to save just one stranger and permissible to do nothing, nor is it equivalent to the disjunctive requirement to save both strangers or do nothing. See Pummer 2019 (286).

10. See Darwall 2010.

11. Here is a more extreme case. Suppose you can do nothing, save the lives of 100 strangers at great cost to yourself, or save these same 100 strangers *and* Z's finger at the same great cost to yourself. Suppose that, even though it is wrong to save the 100 strangers only, the cost is great enough to make it permissible to do nothing. It is not plausible that there is more requiring reason overall to do nothing than there is to save the 100 only.

12. See Barry and Lazar 2022 on the disrespect of allowing harm gratuitously.

13. Even if saving just one stranger allowed *100* others to die gratuitously, it would still seem there isn't more requiring reason overall to do nothing. Suppose you can do nothing, save one stranger at great cost to yourself, or save this same stranger *and* 100 others at the same great cost to yourself. It seems implausible that you are required to (save no one, given that you are not going to save all 101).

14. Horton 2017a. Frowe 2019 (210, 224–225) endorses a similar claim about volunteering to incur costs.

15. What about when you are not willing to incur the great cost of saving at least one of the strangers? Perhaps then (4) is more acceptable as then morality "does not discourage anyone who is willing to save one [stranger] from doing so." Horton 2017a (footnote 8).

16. Rulli 2020 (especially 379–381).
17. Muñoz and Pummer 2022 defend this view.
18. In this example, the excluded alternative of saving both strangers *non-decisively* affects the balance of requiring reasons and permitting reasons among non-excluded alternatives. In other examples, excluded alternatives decisively affect the balance of requiring reasons and permitting reasons among non-excluded alternatives. Suppose you can go to a costume party dressed up (permissible), go to the party without dressing up (wrong), or stay at home (permissible). It is not plausible that it is permissible to (go to the party without dressing up, given that you are not going to go to the party dressed up). Even when going dressed up is an excluded alternative, the fact that it is an *alternative* makes it disrespectful to the host of the party to go without dressing up, so there is more requiring reason overall to stay home than there is to go without dressing up. You are required to (stay home, given that you are not going to go to the party dressed up). Thanks to Joe Horton for this example.
19. As argued in Muñoz and Pummer 2022, the view of conditional permissibility offered in this section is an improvement on the view offered in Pummer 2019. While both it and the Pummer 2019 view imply plausible conditional-permission claims in cases like *Costly No-Conflict*, the Pummer 2019 view has questionable implications in cases like the following (from Kamm 1985): You can keep your promise to meet a friend for lunch (permissible), break your promise by staying home (wrong), or break your promise by saving a stranger's life at great cost to yourself (permissible). Both (3) and the Pummer 2019 view imply that you are required to (save the stranger's life at great cost to yourself, given that you are not going to keep your promise). We might agree with Kamm 1996 (318) that this implication is implausible. The view of conditional permissibility offered in this section avoids this implication if there is a sufficiently strong (cost-based) permitting reason to break your promise by staying home rather than break your promise by saving the stranger's life at great cost to yourself.

4 | PRAISEWORTHINESS

4.1. Are You Blameworthy for Saving the Lesser Number?

In Chapter 3, I considered the following cases.

> *Costly No-Conflict*: Two strangers face a deadly threat. You can do nothing, save one stranger's life at great cost to yourself, or save both their lives at the same great cost to yourself.

> *Costly Conflict*: Three strangers face a deadly threat. You can do nothing, save one stranger's life at great cost to yourself, or save the other two at the same great cost to yourself.

I claimed that, in both cases, it is permissible to do nothing, wrong to save the lesser number, and permissible to save the greater number. I argued that the correct solution to the all or nothing problem does not involve rejecting this claim. And I provided a positive explanation of this claim. In both cases, there is most requiring reason overall to save the greater number, a sufficiently

The Rules of Rescue. Theron Pummer, Oxford University Press. © Oxford University Press 2023.
DOI: 10.1093/oso/9780190884147.003.0005

strong permitting reason to do nothing, and no sufficiently strong permitting reason to save the lesser number.

In this chapter, I present and respond to a new objection to the claim that, in cases like *Costly No-Conflict* and *Costly Conflict*, it is permissible to do nothing, wrong to save the lesser number, and permissible to save the greater number. The objection is brought out by the following argument.

(1) If act *A* is wrong and you lack an excuse for doing *A*, then you are blameworthy for doing *A*.

(2) In cases like *Costly No-Conflict* and *Costly Conflict*, it is wrong to save the lesser number. (As argued in the previous chapter.)

(3) In cases like *Costly No-Conflict* and *Costly Conflict*, you lack an excuse for saving the lesser number.

So,

(4) In cases like *Costly No-Conflict* and *Costly Conflict*, you are blameworthy for saving the lesser number.

However, (4) is contrary to the intuition that (at least in *Costly Conflict*) you are worthy of *praise*, not blame, for saving the lesser number. After all, in doing so, you're saving a stranger at great cost to yourself, and it would have been permissible and blameless for you to save no one. The objection then goes that, since we should reject (4) and accept (1) and (3), we must reject (2).

In this chapter, I respond to this objection. I argue that, instead of rejecting (2), we should reject (1). As with the all or nothing problem, it is worth remembering that readers who favor different solutions can feel free to transpose my arguments from the point of departure, seeing where they lead. For example, those who accept (4) could still accept a set of claims that is very similar to what I defend over the course of the book.

Before turning to my arguments against (1), some preliminaries are needed.

I here take it that to be blameworthy for your conduct is to be *worthy* of blame for it, in that it is appropriate to have a negative attitude toward you for your conduct or in that you deserve discredit for your conduct.[1] You can be blameworthy in such a sense even when blaming you would make things worse (e.g., blaming you in response to your saving the lesser number might lead you to behave less altruistically in the future).

Premise (1) is a commonly held view about the connection between being wrong and being blameworthy. Indeed, some hold that we cannot get a grip on what it means for an act to be wrong unless there is some such connection with blameworthiness.[2] Premise (1) says that you are blameworthy for doing what is wrong, unless special excusing circumstances obtain. Suppose a boulder is hurtling down a hillside and you shove an innocent stranger in its path, thereby killing them. What you do is wrong and blameworthy. But now suppose the boulder is hurtling toward your loved one, and the only way to save them is by shoving the stranger in the boulder's path. Even if the fact that killing this stranger is the only way to save your loved one is not a sufficiently strong permitting reason to kill the stranger, this fact may nonetheless give you a sufficiently strong *excuse* for killing them. If so, then while it is wrong to kill the stranger, you are not blameworthy for doing so.

We can stipulate that in *Costly No-Conflict* and *Costly Conflict* no special excusing circumstances obtain, so that you have no excuse for saving the lesser number. Then we cannot respond to the above objection by rejecting (3).

Next, we need to distinguish between being blameworthy *to some extent* and being blameworthy *overall*. You are blameworthy to some extent for performing an act when you are blameworthy for some aspect of this performance, including your motivation—likewise for being praiseworthy to some extent. You can at once be praiseworthy to some extent for performing an act and blameworthy to some extent for performing this same act. Suppose a hurtling boulder is about to kill a stranger. You can save their life only by releasing the brake on your car so that it will roll down a hill and into the path of the boulder. After deflecting the boulder, your car will foreseeably hit and paralyze another stranger as a side effect. It seems you are praiseworthy to some extent for saving the stranger's life at the significant cost of your car and yet blameworthy to some extent for seriously harming the other stranger (contravening their right not to be harmed) as a foreseen side effect. You are blameworthy *overall* for performing an act when, considering all the praiseworthy and blameworthy aspects of this performance, including your motivations, you are on balance blameworthy for performing this act—likewise for being praiseworthy overall.[3] (My primary focus here is the blameworthiness or praiseworthiness of agents for performing certain acts from certain motivations, as opposed to their blameworthiness or praiseworthiness for having or displaying certain dispositions; sometimes I'll speak of *acts* as being blameworthy or praiseworthy, but this is only shorthand for agents being blameworthy or praiseworthy for performing them.)

I take it that (4), then, is the claim that you are blameworthy *overall* for saving the lesser number. If (4) were merely the claim that you are blameworthy *to some extent* for saving the lesser number, it would not be counterintuitive. Presumably all sorts of acts are blameworthy to *some* extent, and it is only to be expected that saving the lesser number with no sufficiently strong permitting reason or excuse would be too. We could then simply accept (4), and the pressure to reject (2) would disappear.

Since (4) is instead the claim that you are blameworthy *overall* for saving the lesser number, (1) must accordingly be the claim that, if act *A* is wrong and you lack an excuse for doing *A*, then you are blameworthy *overall* for doing *A*. It is (1) so interpreted that I argue against here.[4]

4.2. Wrong yet Praiseworthy: Beneath the Call of Duty

Before coming to counterexamples to (1), consider an example in which an act is wrong yet praiseworthy *to some extent*:

Flight: Two strangers are about to die. You have three alternatives. First, you can do nothing, letting both strangers die. Second, you can rescue in a way that will save one stranger and cause you to miss your nonrefundable international flight. Third, you can rescue in another way that will save both strangers, cause you to miss your flight, *and* muddy your clothes.

(Suppose that, were you to save just one stranger, your motivation would be to avoid the combined cost of missing your flight and muddying your clothes—you're not willing to incur any more cost than that of a missed flight.)[5]

There is most requiring reason overall to save the lives of both strangers, next most requiring reason overall to save just one, and least requiring reason overall to do nothing. It seems morally required to save both, wrong to save just one, and wrong to do nothing. Missing your flight is a significant permitting reason to do nothing, but it is not sufficiently strong next to the requiring reason to save one of the strangers. And muddying your clothes is a permitting reason to save just one stranger, but it is not sufficiently strong next to the requiring reason to save the other stranger.

It is praiseworthy overall to save both strangers. This would involve you paying a significant cost in responding fully to the requiring reasons that are present. When you save just one, you pay a lesser *but still significant* cost in responding inadequately *but still significantly* to the requiring reasons present. Much of what would make it praiseworthy to save both would therefore remain were you to save just one.[6] The wrongness of responding inadequately does not entirely cancel your praiseworthiness. Although in *Flight* saving just one stranger is wrong, it is plausible that you are praiseworthy to some extent for doing so.

This last claim is compatible with (1). In fact, it seems that you are seriously blameworthy for letting one of the strangers die merely in order to avoid muddying your clothes. You are praiseworthy to some extent for saving one stranger but blameworthy to an even greater extent for letting the other die. So, you are blameworthy overall.

But if the scales can tip one way, can they not tip the other? Why couldn't it be that, although you are blameworthy to some extent for saving the lesser number, you are praiseworthy to an even greater extent so that you are praiseworthy overall? It seems that, when responding to the requiring reasons that are present comes at a significant cost to you, the credit you deserve for rising above what there is least requiring reason overall to do can sometimes exceed the discredit you deserve for responding inadequately to the requiring reasons present.[7]

Here is a case of this sort:

Hand: One hundred strangers are about to die, and another stranger, Z, is about to lose their finger. You can do nothing, save just the lives of the 100 strangers at the cost of losing your nondominant hand, or save the 100 and Z's finger at the cost of losing your non-dominant hand *and* stubbing your toe. (Suppose that, were you to save just the lives of the 100 strangers, your motivation would be to avoid the combined cost of losing your hand and stubbing your toe—you're not willing to incur any more cost than that of a lost hand.)

There is most requiring reason overall to save the 100 and Z's finger, next most requiring reason overall to save just the 100, and least requiring reason overall to do nothing. It seems morally required to save the 100 and Z's finger, wrong to save just the 100, and wrong to do nothing. The loss of your non-dominant hand is a significant permitting reason to do nothing, but it is not sufficiently strong next to the requiring reason to save the lives of 100 strangers. (If you doubt this, we can replace the loss of your hand with a somewhat lesser loss, such as the loss of two or three of your fingers; also remember that, like other rescue cases in Chapters 1–5, this case takes place in an imaginary world in which your opportunities to help are very rare.) And stubbing your toe is a permitting reason to save just the 100, but it is not sufficiently strong next to the requiring reason to save Z's finger.

It is praiseworthy overall to save the 100 strangers and Z's finger. It *also* seems praiseworthy overall to save just the 100. The credit you deserve for sacrificing your hand to save the lives of 100 strangers exceeds the discredit you deserve for failing to save Z's finger at the additional cost of stubbing your toe. Although in *Hand* saving just the lives of the 100 strangers is wrong, you are praiseworthy overall for doing it. This plausible claim is incompatible with (1).

4.3. Wrong yet Praiseworthy: Beyond the Call of Duty

In cases like *Hand*, a wrong but overall praiseworthy act is less responsive to the balance of requiring reasons than any permissible alternative—it's in this way "beneath the call of duty." In this section, I argue that cases like *Costly Conflict* provide another kind of counterexample to (1). In these cases, a wrong but overall praiseworthy act is more responsive to the balance of requiring reasons than a permissible alternative—it's in this way "beyond the call of duty."

I begin with a discussion of the motivations for saving the lesser number in cases like *Costly No-Conflict* and *Costly Conflict*. After all, it is not obvious why you *would* save the lesser number in these cases (unlike *Flight* and *Hand*, in *Costly No-Conflict* and *Costly Conflict* it is *no* costlier to you to save the greater number than it is to save the lesser number). And motivations can affect praiseworthiness and blameworthiness.

Although heroic life-saving acts are paradigmatically praise-worthy, they can fail to be praiseworthy—and can be blamewor-thy instead—if they are done for bad motivations. It is plausible that you would be blameworthy for letting one of the strangers in *Costly No-Conflict* die merely because you hate people with their skin color.[8] This would render you blameworthy for saving the lesser number. Bad motivations can similarly render you blame-worthy for doing nothing or for saving the greater number, even though these acts would remain permissible.[9] For example, it is plausible that you are blameworthy for doing nothing if you are motivated by racism rather than a desire to keep your legs. And it is plausible that you are not praiseworthy for saving the greater number if you are motivated by monetary rewards rather than the plights of the imperiled strangers.

There is a motivational difference between *Costly No-Conflict* and *Costly Conflict*. The best motivation available for saving the lesser number in *Costly Conflict* is better than the best motiva-tion available for saving the lesser number in *Costly No-Conflict*.[10] In both cases, the best motivation available for saving the lesser number is partly good and partly bad, and the bad part in *Costly No-Conflict* is worse than the bad part in *Costly Conflict*. It is plau-sible that, while you are blameworthy overall for saving the lesser number in cases like *Costly No-Conflict*, you can be praiseworthy overall for saving the lesser number in cases like *Costly Conflict* (even though saving the lesser number is wrong).

The best sort of motivation available for saving the lesser number in *Costly No-Conflict* is what I call "innumerate altruism." That is, you are moved to *help someone* but are indifferent to how many. Even when fully aware of the plights of each, at any given time you are not moved *more* by more plights than fewer.[11] Equally moved to save just one as you are to save both, your choice to save someone culminates in arbitrarily picking "just one." You do not employ a randomizing procedure (such as a coin toss), but you select arbitrarily between helping someone by saving the lesser number and helping someone by saving the greater number. On this occasion, you happen to go for the lesser number. In addition, your innumerate altruism is anonymous in that you would be equally moved to save just one as you are to save both were the positions of the two strangers swapped. Finally, your innumerate altruistic motivation is quite a powerful one, taking precedence over your strong motivation to keep your legs.

The best sort of motivation available for saving the lesser number in *Costly No-Conflict*—that is, innumerate altruism—is partly good and partly bad. The good part is being motivated to help someone, even at great cost to yourself. The bad part is being indifferent to how many you help. This bad part is pretty bad. It is plausible that, though you are praiseworthy to some extent for saving the lesser number, you are blameworthy overall for doing so. (I take it you're to some extent praiseworthy for saving the lesser number only in that you're to some extent praiseworthy for choosing to *help someone* at great cost to yourself—as you select arbitrarily between helping someone by saving the lesser number and helping someone by saving the greater number.)

The best sort of motivation available for saving the lesser number in *Costly Conflict* is what I call "imbalanced altruism." That is, you are moved by the plights of each and indeed moved more by more plights than fewer, but in conflict cases you are not motivated by an appropriate balance of the plights on each side (you are not motivated in accord with the fact that there is more requiring reason overall to save the two than there is to save the one and no sufficiently strong permitting reason to save the one). In conflict cases with sufficiently similar harms, you might find yourself taking up the perspectives of some of the particular individuals you can help and being moved to save them, whether they happen to belong to the greater number or to the lesser number.[12] Or you might in such conflict cases select arbitrarily between the greater number and the lesser number given that either way you help someone without allowing harm gratuitously. Either sort of imbalanced altruism seems a better motivation than innumerate altruism. Failing to be motivated by an appropriate balance of the plights on each side does not seem as bad as being *indifferent* to the number of people you can help.

It is plausible that, due to this motivational difference, you are blameworthy overall for saving the lesser number in cases like *Costly No-Conflict* but are praiseworthy overall for saving the lesser number out of imbalanced altruism in cases like *Costly Conflict* (even though saving the lesser number is wrong). In such conflict cases, it seems a bigger deal that you heroically save someone than that you fail to appropriately balance conflicting requiring reasons. The credit you deserve for saving the lesser number (rather than saving no one) is greater than the discredit you deserve for saving the lesser number (rather than saving the greater number).

It is plausible that *Costly Conflict* is itself a counterexample to (1), the claim that if act *A* is wrong and you lack an excuse for doing *A*, then you are blameworthy overall for doing *A*. It is plausible that, even though it is wrong to save the lesser number and you lack an excuse for doing so, you are praiseworthy overall, and not blameworthy overall, for saving the lesser number out of imbalanced altruism.

Costly Conflict also provides a plausible example of the more radical phenomenon of being *more* praiseworthy overall for doing an act that is wrong (saving the lesser number) than you would be for doing an alternative that is permissible (saving no one). You are neither praiseworthy nor blameworthy for permissibly saving no one.[13] Even if you were praiseworthy to some extent for saving no one, it is hard to deny that you would be praiseworthy to a much greater extent for heroically saving the one out of imbalanced altruism.

There are further cases in which it is even more plausible that you are praiseworthy overall for performing an act that is wrong and more praiseworthy overall than you would be for performing a permissible alternative. Consider:

10 Plus Conflict: You can do nothing; press a red button, thereby saving the lives of 10 strangers and the life of stranger *X*; or press a green button, thereby saving the lives of these same 10 strangers and the lives of strangers *Y* and *Z*. Pressing either button will also cause you to drop into a fiery pit and die.

In this case, there is more requiring reason overall to press the red button than there is to do nothing and most requiring reason overall to press the green button. But since there is a sufficiently strong permitting reason to do nothing and no sufficiently strong permitting reason to press the red button, it is permissible to do nothing and wrong to press the red button.[14]

The explanation of why you are praiseworthy overall for saving the lesser number out of imbalanced altruism in *Costly Conflict* applies with even greater force in *10 Plus Conflict*. It is a much bigger deal that you super-heroically save the 10 plus X than that you fail to appropriately balance conflicting requiring reasons. So, in this case the credit you deserve for saving the lesser number (rather than saving no one) is much greater than the discredit you deserve for saving the lesser number (rather than saving the greater number). You are praiseworthy overall for pressing the red button, even though this act is wrong. And you are more praiseworthy overall for pressing the red button than you would be for doing nothing, even though it is wrong to press the red button and permissible to do nothing.[15]

In sum, in the previous chapter, I argued for the claim that, in cases like *Costly No-Conflict* and *Costly Conflict*, it is permissible to do nothing, wrong to save the lesser number, and permissible to save the greater number. In this chapter, I presented a new objection to this claim, brought out by the following argument.

(1) If act A is wrong and you lack an excuse for doing A, then you are blameworthy overall for doing A.

(2) In cases like *Costly No-Conflict* and *Costly Conflict*, it is wrong to save the lesser number. (As argued in the previous chapter.)

    (3) In cases like *Costly No-Conflict* and *Costly Conflict*, you
        lack an excuse for saving the lesser number.

So,

    (4) In cases like *Costly No-Conflict* and *Costly Conflict*, you are
        blameworthy overall for saving the lesser number.

However, (4) is contrary to the intuition that (at least in *Costly
Conflict*) you are worthy of *praise*, not blame, for rather heroically
saving the lesser number. The objection then goes that, since we
should reject (4) and accept (1) and (3), we must reject (2).

    In this chapter, I responded to this objection. I argued that,
instead of rejecting (2), we should reject (1). You can be praiseworthy overall rather than blameworthy overall for saving the lesser
number, even though it is wrong to do so (as in cases like *Hand*
and *Costly Conflict*).

Notes

1. For a sample of relevant literature, see Zimmerman 1988, Smith 1991,
   Arpaly 2003, Scanlon 2008, Massoud 2016, Nelkin 2016, and Mason
   2019. I am here setting aside accounts of blameworthiness that are based
   on the effects of blaming. For example, see Arneson 2003a.
2. For example, see Gibbard 1990 (chapter 3), Skorupski 2010 (part III),
   Darwall 2013 (21), and McElwee 2017. Others claim that what it means
   for an act to be wrong is simply that it *mustn't be done* (Parfit 2011,
   chapter 7).

3. What exactly it is to be praiseworthy overall or blameworthy overall depends on what it is to be worthy of praise or blame for performing an act. We might, for instance, conceive of the latter as being deserving of credit or discredit. Then being praiseworthy overall could be a matter of being deserving of more credit than discredit. We might instead conceive of being worthy of praise or blame as being the appropriate target of a positive or negative attitude. Then being praiseworthy overall could be a matter of being the appropriate target of both a positive attitude and a negative attitude, where the positive attitude is relevantly stronger than the negative one or where it is more appropriate to have the positive attitude than it is to have the negative one.

4. This chapter draws upon Pummer 2021.

5. This builds on Massoud's 2016 (692) case in which you can save a stranger's life by missing a nonrefundable international flight. I share her intuition that you are both required to save this stranger's life and praiseworthy for doing so.

6. Praiseworthiness is affected by the costs you incur in responding to reasons. It may also be affected by other factors, such as the extent to which your responsiveness is *exceptional* (relative to your community). For discussion of the latter, see Urmson 1958 and Markovits 2012.

7. The earlier case of sacrificing your car to save a stranger's life while paralyzing another stranger as a side effect isn't a case of this sort, given that there's least requiring reason overall to do this act (it is plausible that requiring reasons not to do harm are relevantly stronger than requiring reasons not to allow harm).

8. This is how McMahan 2018 (94–99) characterizes *Costly No-Conflict*. Similarly, Horton 2017a (94) stipulates that "you are a bad person, and you dislike one of the [strangers]."

9. See Kamm 2007 (132) and Scanlon 2008. For a reply, see Liao 2012.

10. That is, the best motivation available compatible with not having an excuse.

11. Innumerate altruism may be seen as a motivational reflection of these ancient thoughts: "Whosoever preserves a single soul . . . scripture

ascribes as much [merit] to him as if he had preserved a complete world"
(Talmud: Sanhedrin 37a) and "whosoever saves the life of one, it shall be
as if he had saved the life of all of mankind" (Quran 5:32). It may also be
seen as a motivational reflection of the related thought that each person's
life is of infinite moral value so that the moral value of saving just one
person is equivalent to that of saving an arbitrarily large group of people
that contains this same person.

12. Depending on how you encounter those you can help, it may be possible
    to be moved on the basis of a singular thought such as "Lorraine is about
    to be crushed by a boulder." For further discussion, see Pettit 1997 and
    Setiya 2014.

13. We can allow for the possibility that in some cases a permitting reason
    makes an act permissible without making it blameless (see Driver 1992).
    For example, suppose you can costlessly and easily donate your kidney to
    save a stranger's life. It may be permissible yet blameworthy not to donate
    your kidney.

14. Some might hold that, since pressing the red button provides *enough* help,
    there is a sufficiently strong *satisficing* permitting reason to do it, even
    though there is more requiring reason overall to press the green button.
    But, as noted in Chapter 2, when two alternatives are perfectly alike but
    for the fact that one includes allowing $2N$ strangers to die whereas the
    other includes allowing N different strangers to die, it seems there cannot
    be a sufficiently strong satisficing permitting reason to do the former, no
    matter how much help it provides.

15. Similar remarks apply to the following variant of *10 Plus Conflict*, which
    could convince those who believe it is permissible to save the lesser number
    in conflict cases (assuming they agree that there is more requiring reason
    overall to save one stranger's life than there is to save another's legs):

    Equinumerous 10 Plus Conflict: You can do nothing; press a red
    button, thereby saving the lives of 10 strangers and stranger X's
    legs; or press a green button, thereby saving the lives of these
    same 10 strangers and stranger Y's life. Pressing either button
    will also cause you to drop into a fiery pit and die.

5 | DISTANT RESCUES

5.1. Ponds and Charities

In the first four chapters of this book, I defended several claims about the ethics of rescuing strangers. My main task in the remaining chapters is to explore the extent to which similar claims remain defensible across further contexts. I argue that similar claims hold in a range of cases that involve using time and money to help distant strangers (by volunteering, donating to charity, and making a difference with your career).

Here are some of the core claims I have defended so far. Chapter 1: There are strong requiring reasons to save the lives of strangers, and sufficiently strong permitting reasons can prevent these reasons from making it wrong not to save strangers. While it is wrong not to save the stranger in *Costless Rescue*, it is permissible not to save the stranger in *Costly Rescue*. Chapter 2: It is wrong to save the lesser number in cases like *Costless Conflict* as well as in cases like *Costless No-Conflict*. There is more requiring reason overall to save a larger group of strangers than there is to

The Rules of Rescue. Theron Pummer, Oxford University Press. © Oxford University Press 2023.
DOI: 10.1093/oso/9780190884147.003.0006

save a smaller group of different strangers, and there is no sufficiently strong permitting reason to save the smaller group when
the larger group is at least twice as large. Chapter 3: It is wrong to
save the lesser number in cases like *Costly No-Conflict* and *Costly
Conflict*, even though in such cases it is permissible to save no one.
Chapter 4: In cases like *Costly Conflict*, you can be praiseworthy
overall for saving the lesser number (and more praiseworthy overall than you would be for permissibly saving no one), even though
it is wrong to save the lesser number.

The cases discussed so far are "clean" cases in that complications
beyond those mentioned are set aside. Setting aside complications
beyond those mentioned involves supposing that those you can rescue are innocent, that there would be no negative side effects of saving them, and so on. Real-world cases contain many complications.
Moreover, it is natural to imagine that the clean cases discussed so far
involve emergencies in which you can rescue nearby strangers from
immediate threats like hurtling boulders or burning buildings. Such
emergency rescue cases differ in several ways from everyday cases of
using time and money to help distant strangers (by volunteering,
donating to charity, and making a difference with your career). To
appreciate these differences, consider a standard pair of cases.

Pond: You are walking past a shallow pond and see a stranger
drowning in it. You can safely wade in and pull the stranger out,
but this will mean ruining your new clothes. If you do not save
the stranger, they will die.[1]

Charity: There are malaria charities operating in areas of
extreme poverty that save on average one life for every $3000

they receive. You can donate to such a charity right now by visiting a website and entering your credit card details.[2]

Here is a partial list of ways in which cases like *Pond* at least typically differ from cases like *Charity*.

Distance—In cases like *Pond* you are physically near those you can help, whereas in cases like *Charity* you are not.

Salience—In cases like *Pond* the plights of those you can help tend to attract and hold your attention, whereas in cases like *Charity* they do not.

Uniqueness—In cases like *Pond* you alone can help, whereas in cases like *Charity* you are one of many who can help.

Injustice—In cases like *Pond* the plights of those you can help are the result of mere accidents, whereas in cases like *Charity* they are at least partly the result of social injustice.

Community—In cases like *Pond* those you can help are members of your community, whereas in cases like *Charity* they are not. (That someone is a member of your community doesn't imply they are not a stranger.)

Frequency—Cases like *Pond* are rare, whereas cases like *Charity* are very frequent (the latter are constant).

Uncertainty—In cases like *Pond* it is certain that pulling the stranger out will help (and not harm), whereas in cases like *Charity* it is uncertain that donating will help (and not harm).

Diffusion—In cases like *Pond* pulling the stranger out gives a particular stranger a large (100 percent) chance of being helped, whereas in cases like *Charity* donating $3000 at

best gives each of many particular strangers a small chance
of being helped.

Some argue that, due to one or more of these differences, it is
wrong not to help in cases like *Pond* but permissible not to donate
in cases like *Charity*.

Next consider:

Pond v. Charity: You are walking past a shallow pond and see
a stranger drowning in it. You can safely wade in and pull the
stranger out, but this will mean losing $6000 you could donate
to a malaria charity that saves on average one life for every $3000
it receives (if you wade in with the money, it will be destroyed by
the dirty water, and if you try to leave it on the side of the pond,
the wind will blow it in). You can donate this money to the charity only if you let the stranger drown.

Some argue that, due to one or more of the differences between
cases like *Pond* and cases like *Charity*, in *Pond v. Charity* it is permissible, if not required, to save the drowning stranger.

I argue that the "rules of rescue" defended in the previous
four chapters—the core claims about requiring reasons to help
(the greater number) and permitting reasons not to—carry over
to *many* cases of using time and money to help distant strangers (by volunteering, donating to charity, and making a difference with your career). To determine the extent to which these
claims carry over, we need to know which differences between
cases like *Pond* and cases like *Charity* are relevant and how they
are relevant. In Chapters 5–7, I continue working mainly with

clean cases, to determine the moral relevance, if any, of the sorts of factors listed above. In Chapter 8, I turn to real-world implications.

In this chapter, I focus on differences with respect to distance (section 5.2), salience (section 5.3), uniqueness (section 5.4), injustice (section 5.5), uncertainty (section 5.6), and diffusion (section 5.7). In section 5.8, I consider the combination of these factors. Apart from a type of diffusion ("risky diffusion"), I argue that these factors do not make the relevant sort of moral difference. Whether taken individually or in combination, such factors would not make it the case that, while it is wrong not to help in cases like *Pond*, it is permissible not to donate in cases like *Charity*. Nor would they make it the case that it is permissible to help the drowning stranger in cases like *Pond v. Charity*. In Chapter 6, I turn to frequency and related factors and in Chapter 7, community and other special connections.

In all the clean cases discussed throughout the remainder of this chapter, we are to assume the following:

- The rescue situations in question occur very rarely and indeed take place in an imaginary world in which your opportunities to help are very rare—for example, there are no later opportunities to donate to charity (thereby temporarily bracketing *frequency*).
- You will not receive compensation for any costs incurred in rescuing others.[3]
- All the money in your possession is rightfully yours (the fact that it's rightfully yours does not imply that you are permitted to use it as you choose but does imply that there's

an autonomy-based permitting reason of some strength to use it as you choose). For a discussion of property rights, see Chapter 8, section 8.2.

- The strangers you can rescue are not members of your community (thereby temporarily bracketing *community*).
- Complications beyond those mentioned in the case descriptions are set aside.

Two further points to bear in mind:

- While the clean cases discussed in this chapter involve helping by sacrificing money, the sacrifice of money is not *itself* a cost of the relevant sort. What really gives rise to permitting reasons are the sacrifices of well-being, personal projects, or autonomy that correlate with sacrifices of money (though as noted in Chapter 1, not all such sacrifices give rise to permitting reasons not to help).
- While the clean cases discussed in this chapter involve helping strangers by preventing imminent deaths from drowning or being crushed by boulders, real-world cases like *Charity* typically involve helping strangers by providing resources that prevent less imminent deaths. Imminent threats may be salient, but, as I argue in section 5.3, salience does not make a moral difference of the relevant sort. The requiring reason to save a stranger's life by preventing a boulder from crushing them is no stronger than the requiring reason to save a stranger's life by preventing them from being bitten by a malaria-transmitting mosquito, other things (like certainty and magnitude of harm) being equal.[4] We can be required

to help in either of these ways, even if we are not required to provide pure benefits to strangers who are sufficiently well off.

5.2. Distance

Many find it permissible not to donate in cases like *Charity* yet find it wrong not to help at a similar cost in cases like *Pond*. But it is not at all clear that the fact that these cases differ with respect to distance is what explains the intuitive moral difference between them. As the above list suggests, these cases differ with respect to many factors all at once. This makes it difficult to say whether it is distance, one of these other factors, or some combination of factors, that explains the intuitive moral difference. Is it that the drowning stranger in *Pond* is physically near to you or that you are certain that your efforts will result in their actually being saved or that you alone can help them or that their plight is especially salient to you or that such opportunities to rescue are very rare, that makes it seem wrong not to help in *Pond* yet permissible not to help at a similar cost in *Charity*?

To determine whether distance itself explains the moral difference, we need a pair of cases that differ with respect to distance only. These may not be particularly realistic cases since in the real world distance correlates with many other factors, including those listed above. Some have offered pairs of cases in an attempt to show that distance itself makes a moral difference. For example, consider the following.[5]

Near Alone Case: I am walking past a pond in a foreign country that I am visiting. I *alone* see many children drowning in
it, and I alone can save one of them. To save the one, I must put
the $500 I have in my pocket into a machine that then triggers
(via electric current) rescue machinery that will certainly scoop
him out.

Far Alone Case: I *alone* know that in a distant part of a foreign
country that I am visiting, many children are drowning, and
I alone can save one of them. To save the one, all I must do is put
the $500 I carry in my pocket into a machine that then triggers
(via electric current) rescue machinery that will certainly scoop
him out.

It may seem there is a moral difference between these cases. But
while they do control for several factors—including uniqueness,
community, and uncertainty—they still differ with respect to
more than distance. They also differ with respect to salience as
I can *see* the children drowning in the first case but not in the
second.[6]

This is not an unrepresentative example. To my knowledge,
every attempt to offer a pair of cases showing that distance itself
makes a moral difference in fact yields an intuitive difference only
when the cases differ with respect to factors other than distance.[7]
When the cases truly do differ with respect to distance only,
there's no intuitive difference made. I illustrate this by offering a
pair of cases that differ with respect to distance only. Cases purportedly showing that distance itself makes a moral difference fail
to control for confounding factors.

But first, a methodological point. It is important to observe that I am not arguing that, if there's no moral difference between a pair of cases that differ with respect to distance only, then there's no moral difference between *any* pair of cases that differ with respect to distance only.[8] Instead, I am arguing that, since we have not been presented with a pair of cases that truly differ with respect to distance only that yields a moral difference, we should be *skeptical* that there is such a pair of cases. This skepticism, together with a presumption in favor of parsimony, supports the provisional claim that distance does not itself make a moral difference. (Some factors might make a moral difference but not the sort that would make it wrong not to help in cases like *Pond* yet permissible not to donate in cases like *Charity*; I claim distance does not itself make any moral difference, let alone this sort of moral difference.)

Now for the pair of cases that differ with respect to distance only.

Near: While out for a hike in a country you have never been to before, you see on the map of your phone a red dot indicating that there is an emergency about *10 feet* away from you. You tap the dot for a brief description of the situation. It turns out that, on the other side of a tall brick wall, a boulder is hurtling toward stranger A, who is stuck in the boulder's path. You cannot reach A yourself but realize that you are able to save A's life using your phone. For $\$X$ you can tap a button on the screen of your phone that causes a large bulldozer to move in front of the boulder, saving A without doing any damage to the bulldozer. Many other people can similarly help A, but you are certain none of them will.

Far: While out for a hike in a country you have never been to before, you see on the map of your phone a red dot indicating that there is an emergency about *1000 miles* away from you. You tap the dot for a brief description of the situation. It turns out that, on the other side of a tall brick wall, a boulder is hurtling toward stranger *B*. The remaining details are just like those in *Near*.

In *Near* you are physically near those you can help, whereas in *Far* you are not. Nonetheless, if you are required to pay $X to save *A* in *Near*, then you are required to pay a similar amount to save *B* in *Far*.[9]

Next consider the following case, in which you can save either stranger *A* or strangers *B* and *C* and you are physically near *A* but not *B* and *C*.

Near v. Far: While out for a hike in a country you have never been to before, you see on the map of your phone two red dots indicating that there are two emergencies. You tap the dots for brief descriptions of the situations. About 10 feet away on the other side of a tall brick wall, a boulder is hurtling toward stranger *A* (who is stuck in the boulder's path), and about 1000 miles farther away, another boulder is hurtling toward strangers *B* and *C* (who are stuck in this other boulder's path). You cannot reach any of these strangers yourself but realize that, using your phone, you are able to either save *A* for $X or instead save *B* and *C* for $X. You cannot save all three. Many other people can similarly help, but you are certain none of them will.

In *Near v. Far* you are physically near *A* but not *B* and *C*. Nonetheless, it seems wrong to save *A*. The reasons to save *A* are no stronger than the reasons to save *B*. (In a one-on-one conflict between *A* and *B*, you are permitted to save either or required to toss a coin.) And the numbers count: there is more requiring reason overall to save *B* and *C* than there is to save *A* and no sufficiently strong permitting reason to save *A* instead. Even if $X is so large that it is permissible to save no one, it's wrong to save *A*.

5.3. Salience

In cases like *Pond* the plights of those you can help are *salient*—they are such that they tend to attract and hold your attention—whereas in cases like *Charity* they are not.[10] One reason for this is that cases like *Charity* occur very frequently. The plights of those you can help by donating do not stand out to you but blend into the background of your everyday life. By contrast, in all the clean cases discussed throughout this chapter, the rescue scenarios in question occur very rarely. So, all the plights here stand out for being unusual or unexpected. But this is not the only way in which the plights of those you can help in cases like *Pond* are salient. These plights are especially salient because they are so *vividly depicted*. You see the stranger drowning in the pond. By contrast, the plights of those you can help in cases like *Charity* are depicted relatively dully. You merely read about strangers dying of malaria.

Now consider the following pair of cases, which differ with respect to salience only.[11]

Vivid: While out for a hike in a country you have never been to before, you see on the map of your phone a red dot indicating that there is an emergency about 1000 miles away from you. You tap the dot for a brief description of the situation. It turns out that a boulder is hurtling toward stranger *A*, who is stuck in the boulder's path. Immediately after you read this, your phone displays a live video of *A* screaming in terror while trying to escape from the boulder. You find it difficult to put their plight out of your mind. You realize that you can save *A*'s life using your phone. For $X you can tap a button on the screen of your phone that causes a large bulldozer to move in front of the boulder, saving *A* without doing any damage to the bulldozer. Many other people can similarly help *A*, but you are certain none of them will.

Dull: While out for a hike in a country you have never been to before, you see on the map of your phone a red dot indicating that there is an emergency about 1000 miles away from you. You tap the dot for a brief description of the situation. It turns out that a boulder is hurtling toward stranger *B*. The remaining details are just like those in *Vivid*, except that there is no video making *B*'s plight especially salient to you. All you have is the relatively dull depiction, via the brief written description on your phone.

In *Vivid A*'s plight is very salient to you, whereas in *Dull B*'s plight is not very salient to you. Nonetheless, if you are required to pay $X to save *A* in *Vivid*, then you are required to pay a similar amount to save *B* in *Dull*. Salience is like a spotlight that shines on some, leaving others in the dark.[12] It is morally irrelevant that the spotlight shines on *A* but not on *B*. This should have no effect on the reasons to save each.

Next consider:

Vivid v. Dull: While out for a hike in a country you have never been to before, you see on the map of your phone two red dots indicating that there are two emergencies. You tap the dots for brief descriptions of the situations. About 1000 miles away, a boulder is hurtling toward stranger *A* (who is stuck in the boulder's path), and about 1000 miles away in the opposite direction, another boulder is hurtling toward strangers *B* and *C* (who are stuck in this other boulder's path). *A*'s plight is especially salient to you (because it is vividly depicted, as in *Vivid*), but the plights of *B* and *C* are not (because they are dully depicted, as in *Dull*). You realize that, using your phone, you can either save *A* for $X or instead save *B* and *C* for $X. You cannot save all three. Many other people can similarly help, but you are certain none of them will.

Again, the spotlight of salience shines on *A* but not on *B* and *C*, and again, this seems morally irrelevant. It's wrong to save *A*. That *A*'s plight is more salient to you might make it moderately psychologically costly to save *B* and *C* rather than *A*. However, such costs are not permitting reasons to save *A*. At least, the fact that it is moderately psychologically costly not to save *A* because they are in the spotlight of salience couldn't plausibly make it permissible to save *A* rather than *B* and *C* (though perhaps it could excuse you for saving *A*).

Finally, it has been argued that the moral irrelevance of salience can be used to show the moral *relevance* of distance. It has been argued that, since you can permissibly "switch off" whatever makes plights salient in far cases but not in near cases, distance makes a moral difference after all (where switching off salience foreseeably results in not helping).[13] However, when the cases truly differ with respect to distance *only*, distance again fails to make a moral difference. To see this, contrast *Vivid* (in which the stranger you can save is about 1000 miles away from you) with the following:

> *Vivid Plus Near*: While out for a hike in a country you have never been to before, you see on the map of your phone a red dot indicating that there is an emergency about *10 feet* away from you. You tap the dot for a brief description of the situation. It turns out that, on the other side of a tall brick wall, a boulder is hurtling toward stranger *A*, who is stuck in the boulder's path. The remaining details are just like those in *Vivid*.

It seems to me that, for any $X that is the same in both cases, if it is permissible to switch off the video in *Vivid*, then it is also permissible to switch it off in *Vivid Plus Near* (where switching off salience foreseeably results in not helping). For these reasons, I am skeptical that the irrelevance of salience can be used to show the relevance of distance. And I provisionally claim that neither factor itself makes a moral difference.

I have claimed that differences with respect to distance and salience do not make a moral difference. Differences with respect to various other factors (like uniqueness, injustice, or diffusion) may make a moral difference yet still fail to make the *relevant sort* of moral difference. They may still fail to make it the case that, while it is wrong not to help in cases like *Pond*, it is permissible not to donate in cases like *Charity*.

5.4. Uniqueness

Consider the following pair of cases, which differ with respect to *uniqueness* only (i.e., they differ with respect to whether you alone can help or are one of many who can help).[14]

> *Alone*: While out for a hike in a country you have never been to before, you see on the map of your phone a red dot indicating that there is an emergency about 1000 miles away from you. You tap the dot for a brief description of the situation. It turns out that a boulder is hurtling toward stranger *A*, who is stuck in the boulder's path. You realize that you can save *A*'s life using your phone. For $X you can tap a button on the screen of your phone that causes a large bulldozer to move in front of the boulder, saving *A* without doing any damage to the bulldozer. *No one else can help* A.

> *Many*: While out for a hike in a country you have never been to before, you see on the map of your phone a red dot indicating that there is an emergency about 1000 miles away from you. You tap the dot for a brief description of the situation.

It turns out that a boulder is hurtling toward stranger *B*. The remaining details are just like those in *Alone*, except that many other people can similarly help *B*, and you are certain none of them will.

If you are required to pay $X to save *A* in *Alone*, then you are required to pay a similar amount to save *B* in *Many*. Of course, this is not to deny that, if in *Many* the others could chip in and divide the payment of $X equally with you, it would be unfair if you paid the full amount and they paid nothing. In this scenario, they may owe you compensation.

In *Alone v. Many* (the details of which the reader can fill in), you are the only person who can save one stranger, whereas you are one among many others who can save two other strangers (and you are certain no one else will save either of these two other strangers). Even if there is a weak reason to save the one over the two, it seems there is more requiring reason overall to save the two than there is to save the one and no sufficiently strong permitting reason to save the one. It's wrong to save the one.

Finally, even if uniqueness itself does not make a significant moral difference between clean cases like *Alone* and *Many* (or within clean cases like *Alone v. Many*), in many real-world cases uniqueness is correlated with other factors, many of which may well make a significant moral difference. For example, when many people can help, there are often strong reasons to coordinate helping efforts together. In addition, helping those whose plights result from social injustice can create an incentive not to correct the social injustice at the root of the problem.[15] Next, I turn to whether the fact that the plights of those you can help are the result of mere accidents rather than social injustice *itself* makes a significant difference to the permissibility of not helping.

5.5. Injustice

In cases like *Pond* the plights of those you can help are the result of mere accidents, whereas in cases like *Charity* they are at least partly the result of social injustice. Social structures and institutions that cause, enable, or allow extreme poverty are unjust. On some views, our primary responsibility to those in extreme poverty is to work collectively to reform these social structures. And on a subset of these views, our primary collective responsibility to reform unjust social structures is such that we do *not* have *individual* responsibilities to help those whose plights are the result of these social structures (by, e.g., donating to effective charities that fight malaria). We could accordingly hold that, while there are strong requiring reasons to help in cases like *Pond*, there aren't in cases like *Charity*.[16]

But consider the following cases.

Injustice: While out for a hike in a country you have never been to before, you see on the map of your phone a red dot indicating that there is an emergency about 1000 miles away from you. You tap the dot for a brief description of the situation. It turns out that a boulder is hurtling toward stranger *A*, who is stuck in the boulder's path. *A*'s plight is the result of unjust institutions and social structures: *A* is one of many workers living in extreme poverty who, to provide for themselves and their families, have to take a risky route to and from work each day. Along this route, falling boulders regularly kill workers. Although we could collectively reform the unjust social structures and thereby prevent these tragic deaths, it is very rare that any of us could save an individual worker from a falling boulder (it is as rare as cases like *Pond*). However, you realize that you can save A's life using your phone. For $X you can tap a button on the screen of your phone that causes a large bulldozer to move in front of the boulder, saving A without doing any damage to the bulldozer. Many other people can similarly help A, but you are certain none of them will.

Accident: While out for a hike in a country you have never been to before, you see on the map of your phone a red dot indicating that there is an emergency about 1000 miles away from you. You tap the dot for a brief description of the situation. It turns out that a boulder is hurtling toward stranger B. The remaining details are just like those in *Injustice*, except that B's plight is the result of a mere accident (rather than social injustice)—B has to take the same risky route to work as A, but on this occasion, B isn't on the risky route.

In *Accident* the plights of those you can help are the result of mere accidents, whereas in *Injustice* they are the result of social injustice. Nonetheless, if you are required to pay $X to save B in *Accident*, then you are required to pay (at least) a similar amount to save A in *Injustice*.[17]

In *Accident v. Injustice* (the details of which the reader can fill in), one stranger's plight is the result of a mere accident, whereas the plights of two others are the result of social injustice. It seems that there is more requiring reason overall to save the two than there is to save the one and no sufficiently strong permitting reason to save the one. It's wrong to save the one.

5.6. Uncertainty

A further difference is that in clean cases like *Pond* it is certain that pulling the stranger out of the pond will help, whereas in real-world cases like *Charity* it is uncertain that donating will help. This difference matters morally. There is more requiring reason overall to give someone a 100 percent chance of being saved than there is to give them a 50 percent chance of being saved (here and elsewhere I take "chance" to refer to subjective probability or degree of certainty).[18] Nonetheless, if in *Pond* pulling the stranger out of the pond gave them only a 50 percent chance of being saved, you would still be required to do so. The fact that in cases like *Charity* it is uncertain that donating will help does not imply you are not required to donate.

Relatedly, in *Pond* there is no chance that pulling the stranger out of the pond will cause harm to anyone, whereas in real-world cases like *Charity* there is a non-negligible chance that donating will cause harm to some individuals.[19] This difference matters morally. There is a requiring reason not to bring about a non-negligible chance of causing harm, and it's stronger the greater the chance. Nonetheless, if in *Pond* giving the drowning stranger a 75 percent chance of being saved had the side effect of creating a 1 percent chance of someone else dying, it still seems you would be required to do this. The fact that in cases like *Charity* there is a non-negligible chance that donating will cause harm does not imply you are not required to donate.

These quick remarks about uncertainty are meant to show that the fact that real-world cases like *Charity* involve uncertainty about whether your act will help or harm does not by itself prevent core claims from Chapters 1–4 from carrying over to real-world cases of using time and money to help distant strangers. Undoubtedly, there is a significant range of real-world cases like *Charity* in which the chance of helping is low enough and the chance of harming is high enough that there is more requiring reason overall not to donate to the charity in question than there is to donate to it. But not all charities are so bad, and some are very good. (For further discussion, see Chapter 8, section 8.1.)

5.7. Diffusion

Even if in cases like *Charity* there is a 99 percent chance that donating will save someone or other, there will typically be no one *in particular* who gets such a large chance of being saved. When you give $3000 to a charity that saves on average one life for every $3000 it receives, that will typically result in small chances of being saved that are diffused over a large number of particular strangers rather than a large chance of being saved concentrated on any particular stranger. There are at least three importantly different ways that chances of being saved can be diffused over particular individuals. I refer to them as *closed* diffusion, *open* diffusion, and *risky* diffusion.[20]

The following three rescue cases illustrate each type of diffusion in turn.

Closed Diffusion: While out for a hike in a country you have never been to before, you see on the map of your phone a red dot indicating that there is an emergency about 1000 miles away from you. You tap the dot for a brief description of the situation. There are 300 boulders about to crush 300 strangers, one boulder per stranger. There are 300 bulldozers that can stop the boulders, one bulldozer per boulder. If activated, a bulldozer will move into the path of its corresponding boulder, bringing about a 99 percent chance of stopping it. For $X you can tap a button on the screen of your phone that will certainly activate *one or another* of the bulldozers, and there is an equal (1/300) chance of any bulldozer in particular being the one to get activated. *Each particular stranger would get a 1/300 (times 99/100) chance of being saved, and there is a 99 percent chance that some stranger or other would be saved.* Many other people can similarly help these strangers, but you are certain none of them will.

Open Diffusion: As in *Closed Diffusion*, except now there are 10 times as many strangers, boulders, and bulldozers (3000 of each) and paying $X will not certainly activate one or another of the bulldozers. Instead, paying $X will give *each* particular bulldozer an independent 1/300 chance of being activated, and, if activated, a bulldozer will move into the path of its corresponding boulder, bringing about a 99 percent chance of stopping it. While each particular stranger would thus get a 1/300 (times 99/100) chance of being saved, there is a chance no one would be saved. But there is a greater than 99 percent chance that *at least* one stranger or another would be saved (and a good chance that more than one would be saved).

Risky Diffusion: As in *Closed Diffusion*, except now a single boulder is about to crush all 300 strangers, who are together stuck in its path. You can pay $X to bring about a 1/300 chance that a bulldozer will block the boulder, saving all these strangers. While each particular stranger would get a 1/300 chance of being saved, there is a very good (299/300) chance *no one* would be saved.

In *Closed Diffusion* and *Open Diffusion*, paying $X is almost certain to save at least one stranger or another, but in *Risky Diffusion*, paying $X is almost certain to save no one. Now contrast these different cases of diffusion with the following case in which you can concentrate a large chance of being saved on a particular stranger.

Concentration: As in *Closed Diffusion*, except now you are only able to help *one of the strangers in particular*. For $X you can bring about a 99 percent chance that this particular stranger is saved.

Even if it makes a moral difference whether one particular individual gets a 99 percent chance of being saved or many particular individuals each get a small chance of being saved so that there is a 99 percent chance that *someone* will be saved, it still seems that, if you are required to pay $X to help in *Concentration*, then you are required to pay a similar amount to help in *Closed Diffusion*.

Similarly, in *Concentration v. Closed Diffusion* (the details of which the reader can fill in), where you can either pay $X to give one particular stranger a 99 percent chance of being saved or instead pay $X to bring about a 99 percent chance of two strangers being saved, though no two in particular (each particular stranger gets a small chance of being saved), it seems there is more requiring reason overall to do the latter and no sufficiently strong permitting reason to do the former.[21]

It is not clear how many real-world cases like *Charity* are like *Closed Diffusion* with respect to diffusion. At least many such real-world cases are more like *Open Diffusion*. For example, suppose that in *Charity* your $3000 is used to give each of 3000 people an insecticide-treated net, thereby giving each of them an independent 1/300 chance of being saved from dying of malaria. This brings about a greater than 99 percent chance that at least one person or other would be saved.

It seems that if you are required to pay $X to help in *Concentration*, then you are required to pay (at least) a similar amount to help in *Open Diffusion*, when in the latter there is a greater than 99 percent chance that $X will result in at least one person or other being saved. Similarly, in *Concentration v. Open Diffusion* (the details of which the reader can fill in), where you can either pay $X to give one particular stranger a 99 percent chance of being saved or instead pay $X to bring about a 99 percent chance of at least two strangers being saved, it seems there is more requiring reason overall to do the latter and no sufficiently strong permitting reason to do the former.

Some real-world cases like *Charity* are more like *Risky Diffusion*. For example, suppose that in *Charity* your $3000 has a small (1/

300) chance of making the difference to whether a humanitarian operation that would save many lives goes ahead. Your donation could have the *expected value* of saving one stranger, if it brings about a 1/300 chance that 300 strangers are saved.[22]

There remains a strong requiring reason to help in cases like *Risky Diffusion*—and, clearly, if you could *costlessly* bring about a 1/300 chance of saving 300 strangers, it would be wrong not to do so. Nonetheless, it does seem plausible that, for some $X, you can be required to pay $X to help in *Concentration* yet permitted not to pay this amount (or similar) to help in *Risky Diffusion*. This is so even when the expected value of helping is significantly greater in the latter case. Similarly, in *Concentration v. Risky Diffusion* (the details of which the reader can fill in), it seems plausible that it is permissible or even required to pay $X to give one particular stranger a 99 percent chance of being saved instead of paying $X to bring about a 1/300 chance of saving 600 strangers, even though the latter has more than twice the expected value in terms of lives saved. (Such claims may be even more intuitive when the chance of saving is much lower—as in a 1/300,000,000 chance of saving 600,000,000.)[23]

At the same time, it is plausible that there is some number N so that it is *not* permissible to pay $NX to give each of N particular strangers a 99 percent chance of being saved instead of paying $NX to bring about N separate 1/300 chances of saving 600 strangers (where there's a different group of 600 strangers for each separate 1/300 chance). Cases in which you can at once play sufficiently many separate lotteries, each like the one in *Risky Diffusion*, are more like *Open Diffusion*.

In the real world, many cases like *Charity* will be like *Open Diffusion*, some will be like *Risky Diffusion*, and many will involve a mixture of these two types of diffusion (e.g., suppose your donation has a small chance of making the difference to whether many insecticide-treated nets are delivered, where each net would provide a different stranger with an independent small chance of being saved from death). Suppose it is the case that, for some $X, you can be required to pay $X to help in *Concentration* yet permitted not to pay this amount (or similar) to help in *Risky Diffusion*. Then, to the extent that cases like *Charity* are like *Risky Diffusion*, there will be a corresponding gap between the most you can be required to pay in cases like *Pond* and the most you can be required to pay in cases like *Charity*.

5.8. Combined Cases

So far, I have argued that differences with respect to distance, salience, uniqueness, injustice, closed diffusion, and open diffusion do not individually make the relevant sort of moral difference. That is, taken individually, such factors would not make it the case that, while it is wrong not to help in cases like *Pond*, it is permissible not to donate in cases like *Charity*. Nor would they make it the case that it is permissible to help the drowning stranger in cases like *Pond v. Charity*.

Even if these factors do not individually make the relevant sort of moral difference, they could in theory *collectively* do so. But, in fact, they do not. To see that they do not collectively make the relevant sort of moral difference, consider the following pair of cases, which differ with respect to distance, salience, uniqueness, injustice, and open diffusion, and equally involve uncertainty.

NearPlus: While out for a hike in a country you have never been to before, you see on the map of your phone a red dot indicating that there is an emergency about 10 feet away from you. You tap the dot for a brief description of the situation. It turns out that, on the other side of a tall brick wall, a boulder is hurtling toward stranger A. Immediately after you read this, your phone displays a live video of A screaming in terror while trying to escape from the boulder. You find it difficult to put their plight out of your mind. You realize that you can save A's life using your phone. For $X you can tap a button on the screen of your phone that will cause a large bulldozer to move in front of the boulder, bringing about a 99 percent chance of saving A. No one else can help A.

FarPlus: While out for a hike in a country you have never been to before, you see on the map of your phone a red dot indicating that there is an emergency about 1000 miles away from you. You tap the dot for a brief description of the situation. There are 3000 boulders about to crush 3000   strangers, one boulder per stranger. As in *Injustice*, their plight is the result of unjust institutions and social structures, though it is very rare for any of us to be able to help save those whose plights result from these structures. You realize that you can help. As in *Open Diffusion*, for $X you can tap a button on the screen of your phone that will give each of these 3000 strangers an independent $1/300$ (times $99/100$) chance of being saved so that there is a greater than 99 percent chance that at least one stranger or other will be saved (and a good chance that more than one will be saved). Many other people can similarly help these strangers, but you are certain none of them will.

It seems that if you are required to pay $X to help in *NearPlus*, then you are required to pay (at least) a similar amount to help in *FarPlus*. Similarly, in *NearPlus v. FarPlus* (the details of which the reader can fill in), where you can either pay $X to give one particular stranger a 99 percent chance of being saved or instead pay $X to bring about a 99 percent chance of at least two other strangers being saved, it seems there is more requiring reason overall to do the latter and no sufficiently strong permitting reason to do the former. It's wrong to save the one.

Differences with respect to distance, salience, uniqueness, injustice, closed diffusion, and open diffusion do not individually or collectively make the relevant sort of moral difference. These factors would not prevent the core claims defended in Chapters 1–4 from carrying over to real-world cases of using time and money to help distant strangers by volunteering, donating to charity, and making a difference with your career.

Notes

1. From Singer 1972.
2. See https://www.givewell.org/.
3. On emergency rescues and insurance, see Barry and Øverland 2013, Haydar and Øverland 2019, and Sterri and Moen 2021.

4. Does it matter that, in saving a stranger from a boulder, you *divert a threat*, whereas in saving a stranger from malaria, you *provide a resource* (like an insecticide-treated net or antimalarial medicine)? Those who think this matters can adjust my rescue cases so that they fall on the "providing resources" side of this distinction. For instance, suppose a stranger spontaneously develops a heart condition and needs their aspirin within a minute to live. They cannot reach their aspirin, but you can remotely turn on a fan that blows it into their hand. Adjusting my rescue cases in this way will not affect the main arguments of this book.

5. Quoted from Kamm 2000 (657) and Kamm 2007 (348).

6. Kamm 2000 (664–666) is aware of this fact and proceeds to argue that, because salience can permissibly be "switched off" in far cases but not in near cases, distance does make a moral difference after all. I respond to this argument at the end of the next section.

7. For another example, see Woollard's 2015 (134) *Door* and *Distant Pond (Many Saviours)*. These cases differ with respect to more than distance— they differ with respect to community and salience, among other factors (see Pummer and Crisp 2020). In addition, some cases offered to show that distance does *not* itself make a moral difference are also flawed. For example, Unger 1996 (34) offers a pair of *Charity*-like cases that differ with respect to distance (*Envelope* and *Bungalow Compound*). He claims that, because it seems permissible not to help in each case, distance does not make an intuitive moral difference. First, it is not clear that these cases differ with respect to distance only. Second, both *Charity*-like cases are very frequent, which may explain the intuition that it is permissible not to help in each case. Unger 1996 (34–35) also offers a pair of *Pond*-like cases that differ with respect to distance (*Sedan* and *CB Radios*). He claims that, because it seems wrong not to help in each case, distance does not make an intuitive moral difference. But both *Pond*-like cases are very rare, and the plights of those you can help are especially salient to you. These factors may explain the intuition that it is wrong not to help in each case.

8. See Kamm 1983 on "contextual interaction" and Kagan 1988 on the "additive fallacy."

9. As Kamm 2000 (661–664) and Woollard 2015 (135–136, 151–152) note, there are multiple ways of measuring distance or nearness. One might claim that, even though A is only 10 feet away, the fact that the brick wall prevents you from directly reaching A makes it the case that A is not near. It would then seem that physical nearness is no longer the factor being appealed to but a sort of nearness-related *salience* or *personal encounter* (see section 5.3).

   On Kamm's view, it is not only physical nearness to you of those you can help that matters but also physical nearness to you of *threats to* those you can help and physical nearness to *means of helping that belong to you* of those you can help. Variants of *Near* and *Far* also cast doubt on the moral relevance of these other sorts of physical nearness. For example, suppose that in *Near Threat* a boulder—the threat—is currently 10 feet away from you on the other side of the tall brick wall and will crush A (who is far away from you) if you do not press the button on your phone within the next minute. If you are required to pay $\$X$ to save A in *Near Threat*, then you are required to pay a similar amount to save B in *Far Threat* (in which both B and the boulder are far away from you).

10. Unger's 1996 (28–29) notion of *conspicuousness* is the same as Kamm's 2000 (664) notion of *salience*.

11. This isn't completely accurate, as these cases also differ with respect to *personal encounter* of the sort had when you see, hear, or communicate with another person. Salience and personal encounter can come apart, but in the cases I consider here they come together (I assume watching a live video of someone is one way to relevantly "see" them). For discussion of personal encounter and similar, see Kamm 2000 (665), Woollard 2015, Miller 2020, Pummer and Crisp 2020, Temkin 2022 (65–81), and Setiya forthcoming. In some cases of personal encounter, an imperiled person (nonverbally) *requests help from you in particular*. Arguably, there is a requiring reason to respond to such directed requests for help. Sometimes you can respond to someone's request for help without helping them, for

example, by explaining to them why you must instead help a larger group of people. Other times the only way you can respond to someone's request for help is by actually helping them. Arguably, there is then somewhat more requiring reason overall to help them than there is to help someone else who has not requested help from you in particular, other things being equal. But it seems there is more requiring reason overall to save two strangers who have not requested help from you than there is to save one other who has (and no sufficiently strong permitting reason to save the one).

12. This is how the psychologist Bloom 2016 characterizes empathy.

13. This argument is from Kamm 2000 (665–666). It seems to me that the cases she appeals to either contain confounds or are underdescribed in ways that encourage imagining them with confounds. For example, she does not control for costs correlated with frequency. It is much costlier to stay switched on to a device that detects very frequently occurring opportunities to help distant strangers than it is to stay switched on to a device that detects very rarely occurring opportunities to help near strangers (for further discussion, see Chapter 6).

14. See Murphy 1993 and Woollard 2015 (136).

15. On coordination issues, see Temkin 2019, Clark and Pummer 2019, and Collins 2019. For discussion of "systemic change" objections to humanitarian aid, see Berkey 2018, Ashford 2018, Dietz 2019, and Gabriel and McElwee 2019.

16. For discussion, see Kamm 2000 (668–670), Herman 2012 (408–409), and Sinclair 2018 (51–52). According to Ashford 2018, there is *both* a primary collective responsibility to reform the unjust social structures that perpetuate extreme poverty *and* an individual responsibility to help those living in extreme poverty by donating to effective charities.

17. On some views, we have even stronger reasons to help others when their plights are the result of social injustices (to which we have contributed or from which we have benefited). For discussion, see Barry and Øverland 2016, Woollard 2019, and Crisp and Pummer 2020.

18. Although I take "chance" to refer to subjective probability, I believe most, if not all, of my arguments work on an objective interpretation. On interpretations of probability, see Hájek 2019.

19. For discussion, see Wenar 2011, Deaton 2013 (chapter 7), Pummer 2016b, Temkin 2019, MacAskill 2019b, and Côté and Steuwer 2022.

20. The "closed" and "open" labels are from Tadros 2013. "Risky" diffusion is a misnomer in that all types of diffusion involve risk or chance. But in the case of risky diffusion, there is a *large chance that no one will be saved* (and a small chance that everyone will be). It is in this sense a risky type of diffusion.

21. For further discussion, see Unger 1996, Hare 2012, Otsuka 2015, Frick 2015, Horton 2017b, Gordon-Solmon 2019, Mogensen 2019, and Kumar unpublished. Unger 1996 (51–52) offers a pair of *Charity*-like cases that differ with respect to diffusion (*Envelope* and *Very Special Relations Fund*). He claims that, because it seems permissible not to help in each case, diffusion does not make an intuitive moral difference. First, it is not clear to me that it is permissible not to help in *Very Special Relations Fund*. Second, insofar as both these *Charity*-like cases are very frequent, that could be what makes it seem permissible not to help in each case. Unger 1996 (52) also offers a pair of *Pond*-like cases that differ with respect to diffusion (*Sedan* and *Vintage Boat*). He claims that, because it seems wrong not to help in each case, diffusion does not make an intuitive moral difference. But both *Pond*-like cases are very rare, and the plights of those you can help are especially salient to you. These factors may explain the intuition that it is wrong not to help in each case.

22. On expected value and making a difference, see Kagan 2011, Nefsky 2019, Budolfson 2019, and Budolfson and Spears 2019.

23. We might defend such claims about cases like *Concentration*, *Risky Diffusion*, and *Concentration v. Risky Diffusion* by appealing to the permissibility or appropriateness of risk aversion. For discussion, see Buchak 2013, Monton 2019, Snowden 2019, and Thoma 2019.

6 | FREQUENT RESCUES

6.1. Frequency

In the previous chapter, I looked at the following pair of cases:

Pond: You are walking past a shallow pond and see a stranger drowning in it. You can safely wade in and pull the stranger out, but this will mean ruining your new clothes. If you do not save the stranger, they will die.

Charity: There are malaria charities operating in areas of extreme poverty that save on average one life for every $3000 they receive. You can donate to such a charity right now by visiting a website and entering your credit card details.

I also considered:

Pond v. Charity: You are walking past a shallow pond and see a stranger drowning in it. You can safely wade in and pull the stranger out, but this will mean losing $6000 you could donate

The Rules of Rescue. Theron Pummer, Oxford University Press. © Oxford University Press 2023.
DOI: 10.1093/oso/9780190884147.003.0007

to a malaria charity that saves on average one life for every $3000 it receives (if you wade in with the money, it will be destroyed by the dirty water, and if you try to leave it on the side of the pond, the wind will blow it in). You can donate this money to the charity only if you let the stranger drown.

Some argue that, due to one or more differences between cases like *Pond* and cases like *Charity*, it is wrong not to help in cases like *Pond*, permissible not to donate in cases like *Charity*, and permissible (if not also required) to help the drowning stranger in cases like *Pond v. Charity*. In the previous chapter, I focused on differences with respect to distance, salience, uniqueness, injustice, and diffusion. On the basis of several "clean" cases—which bracket various complications—I argued that these factors do not make the relevant sort of moral difference ("risky diffusion" is an exception). Whether taken individually or in combination, such factors would not make it the case that, while it is wrong not to help in cases like *Pond*, it is permissible not to donate in cases like *Charity*. Nor would they make it the case that it is permissible to help the drowning stranger in cases like *Pond v. Charity*.

In this chapter, I turn to another difference between cases like *Pond* and cases like *Charity* that may seem to matter. There is a difference with respect to *frequency*: while cases like *Pond* are rare, cases like *Charity* are very frequent. You can be reasonably confident that you will not find yourself in a case like *Pond* at any point next week, month, or year. By contrast, you can be reasonably confident that, at every minute from now until you die, you will be in a case like *Charity*—you will be able to donate to charities that prevent significant harms from befalling distant strangers.

I argue that frequency matters in one way but not in another. On the one hand, it matters whether you find yourself in a world in which opportunities to help strangers at cost to yourself are very frequent or very rare. (Recall that we've been supposing that rescue cases take place in an imaginary world in which your opportunities to help are very rare.) In section 6.2, I look at a case in which individual opportunities to help are like *Pond* (with respect to distance, salience, uniqueness, injustice, and diffusion) yet arise very frequently. In this imagined case, the lifetime cost to you of helping every time you can would be extreme. It seems you are not required to take every individual opportunity to help, even if you are required to take some. In section 6.3, I develop a view that explains this claim. According to this view, lifetime features amplify permitting reasons not to incur costs in saving strangers.

On the other hand, the relative frequency of specific types of opportunities to help does not itself make a difference to requiring reasons or permitting reasons. In section 6.4, I argue that considerations of cost and autonomy correlated with frequency nonetheless explain how it is sometimes permissible not to respond to a frequently occurring opportunity to help when it would have been wrong not to respond to an otherwise similar rarely occurring opportunity to help. In section 6.5, I draw out the implications for cases like *Pond v. Charity*.

6.2. With Many Opportunities to Rescue Come Many Requiring Reasons

In the last section of the previous chapter, I looked at a case that is as rare as *Pond* but is like *Charity* with respect to distance, salience, uniqueness, injustice, and diffusion (*FarPlus*). And I compared it with an equally rare case that is like *Pond* with respect to distance, salience, uniqueness, injustice, and diffusion (*NearPlus*). To determine what frequency itself contributes, consider a case in which individual opportunities to help are like *NearPlus* yet arise very frequently.[1]

> *Frequent NearPlus*: Upon your arrival in a country you have never been to before, your trusty phone informs you that a series of accidents is about to occur. For the indefinite future, boulder upon boulder will threaten stranger upon stranger.
>
> Once every minute, you will see on the map of your phone a red dot indicating that there is an emergency about 10 feet away from you. On the other side of a tall brick wall, a boulder will be hurtling toward a stranger. Your phone will then display a live video of the stranger screaming in terror while trying to escape from the boulder. You will find it difficult to put their plight out of your mind. For $3000, you will be able to tap a button on the screen of your phone that will cause a large bulldozer to move in front of the boulder, bringing about a 99 percent chance of saving the stranger. No one else will be able to help the imperiled stranger.
>
> Three thousand dollars per minute adds up quickly (around $4.3 million per day!). Fortunately, for the rest of your life, you will receive $3000 for every minute you stand on a large green button. This is the only way you can acquire money. There are no other ways of helping strangers—for example, you cannot ever donate to charities. Apart from taking breaks to do what you must in order to survive, you could spend the remainder of your life saving strangers from being crushed by boulders. You would

not enjoy standing on the green button all day long, day after day. And, while standing on the green button, you would be incrementally missing out on things that make life worth living. You are, however, able to switch off the boulder-emergency notifications on your phone. At any point, you can take a break or walk away from the rescue situation entirely (taking any money with you that you acquired from standing on the green button). Of course, either will mean letting more strangers die.

At every minute you have at least $3000, it would seem the requiring reason to save a stranger is strong enough to require you to pay $3000 to give them a 99 percent chance of being saved. The permitting reason to keep the $3000 for yourself does not seem sufficiently strong to permit you to let them die. And, at least whenever you are about to run out of money, it would seem the requiring reason to save a stranger is strong enough to require you to stay on the green button for a minute to get enough money to do so. The permitting reason to have the minute to yourself does not seem sufficiently strong to let someone die. The balance of requiring reasons and permitting reasons present at each time seems to imply that you are required to save as many strangers as possible, spending the remainder of your life standing on the green button and paying out increments of $3000 whenever you can, taking breaks to do what you must in order to survive.

Some may be prepared to accept this implication, even if it is counterintuitive. I find it difficult to believe you would be required to save as many strangers as possible, given the extreme lifetime cost of doing so. Moreover, whether you spend the remainder of your life saving as many strangers as possible presumably makes a very big difference to how your life unfolds. It is plausible that considerations of cost and autonomy make it permissible not to spend the remainder of your life saving strangers. While you are not required to take every individual opportunity to help, it would be wrong not to take *any* individual opportunity to help. You are required to help sometimes.

At what point is it permissible not to help? There are familiar issues of cutoffs here. Any precise cutoff seems arbitrary—why draw the line at saving 100,000 strangers and not 99,999? On the other hand, it may prove difficult to make sense of the idea that there is *no* precise cutoff but only a vague range instead. I do not attempt to resolve these issues here. I assume that some cutoffs—precise or not—are acceptable.[2]

Still, what could explain why you are required to help on some occasions but not required to help on all? And what could explain when you are required to help?

According to one possible view, the requiring reasons to save strangers *diminish* in strength as you save more and more over time. For example, there is a strong requiring reason to save the first stranger, a slightly weaker requiring reason to save the second, and so on, and only a vanishingly weak requiring reason to save the hundred thousandth stranger. So, at least by the time you get to the hundred thousandth stranger, the weak permitting reason not to stand on the green button for a minute is sufficiently strong next to this vanishingly weak requiring reason to help, and thus you are permitted to walk away. This possible view can capture the plausible claim that, while you are not required to take every individual opportunity to help in *Frequent NearPlus*, you are required to help sometimes.

Nonetheless, we should reject this view. Suppose that saving all the strangers prior to the hundred thousandth is costless to you and makes no difference to how your life unfolds. For example, consider a variant of *Frequent NearPlus* in which you can press a button so that your phone will at no cost to you save one stranger per minute until you have saved 99,999. Once you have saved 99,999 strangers, you can incur a minute of inconvenience to save another stranger. The view according to which the requiring reasons to save strangers diminish in strength as you save more and more over time has the implausible implication that you are permitted not to save the hundred thousandth stranger.

The view could avoid this implication if it were revised so that requiring reasons to save strangers diminish in strength as you save more and more over time *at costs* to yourself. But it would be odd if requiring reasons to save individual strangers diminished when saving each is costly but not when saving each is costless. More fundamentally, the very idea that these requiring reasons diminish in strength seems odd. The requiring reason to save the hundred thousandth stranger seems no weaker than the requiring reason to save the first, whether or not saving each comes at a cost to you.

According to another possible view, there are no requiring reasons to save any of the individual strangers in *Frequent NearPlus* but only a requiring reason to *save enough* of them.[3] This view can also capture the plausible claim that, while you are not required to take every individual opportunity to help in *Frequent NearPlus*, you are required to help sometimes. And it can do so without implying that the requiring reason to save the hundred thousandth stranger is any weaker than the requiring reason to save the first.

Nonetheless, we should reject this view too. First, it is simply implausible that there are no requiring reasons to save any of the individual strangers in *Frequent NearPlus*. There is clearly a requiring reason to save the individual stranger in *NearPlus* (taken as occurring in an imaginary world in which your opportunities to help are very rare). And *Frequent NearPlus* is just a series of such opportunities to rescue. It seems that, if there is a strong requiring reason to save the individual stranger in *NearPlus*, then there is an equally strong requiring reason to save each of the individual strangers in *Frequent NearPlus*.

Second, consider a variant of *Frequent NearPlus* in which you can save any number of strangers without incurring any cost or making any difference to how your life unfolds. The view according to which there is only a requiring reason to save enough strangers has the implausible implication that, once you have saved enough, you can permissibly walk away, allowing the rest of the strangers to die. Moreover, this implication cannot plausibly be avoided by claiming that there are requiring reasons to save each individual stranger when saving any number is costless but not when saving each comes at a cost. Although the costs to you of helping can make it the case that you are not required to help, it is not plausible that they can make it the case that there are no requiring reasons to help—requiring reasons to save lives do not disappear when costs appear. If there is a requiring reason to save each individual stranger in the variant of *Frequent NearPlus* in which saving any number is costless, then there is a requiring reason to save each individual stranger in the original variant of the case in which saving each comes at a (slight) cost.

Our problem about *Frequent NearPlus* remains. What could explain why you are required to help on some occasions but not required to help on all? What could explain when you are required to help? The problem cannot be solved by fiddling with requiring reasons to save strangers, for example, by appealing to requiring reasons of diminishing strength. There is an equally strong requiring reason to save each individual stranger.

6.3. Lifetime Features that Amplify Permitting Reasons

According to a more promising type of view, *permitting reasons* not to save strangers at a cost to yourself *increase* in strength as you incur a greater and greater lifetime cost in the course of saving more and more (and they increase in strength more, the less lifetime well-being you're left with as a result of saving strangers). For example, we might hold that in *Frequent NearPlus* there is a very weak permitting reason not to save the first stranger, a slightly stronger permitting reason not to save the second, and so on. There is a very strong permitting reason not to save the hundred thousandth stranger. At *that* point, avoiding the slight inconvenience of standing on the green button for a minute is a sufficiently strong permitting reason even next to the strong requiring reason to save a stranger's life. So, at least by the time you get to the hundred thousandth stranger, you are permitted to walk away.

This view is not to be confused with the empirical claim that, as you sacrifice more money and time, it will typically become *costlier* to you in terms of well-being to sacrifice still more money and time, in accordance with the law of diminishing marginal utility. The view in question is instead that, the more well-being you've sacrificed in total over your life (in the course of saving strangers), the stronger the permitting reasons not to sacrifice still more. Thus, even making the simplifying assumption that in *Frequent NearPlus* the cost of saving the first stranger is equivalent to the cost of saving the hundred thousandth stranger, the view implies that the permitting reason not to save the hundred thousandth stranger is stronger.

Whether the lifetime cost incurred in saving strangers yields a sufficiently strong permitting reason not to save a stranger's life at a slight cost may depend on what particular costs this lifetime cost is comprised of. In *Frequent NearPlus*, the minute-long intervals of inconvenience on the green button involve the particular costs of incrementally missing out on things that make life worth living. It seems plausible that a lifetime cost comprised of such particular costs *can* yield a sufficiently strong permitting reason not to save a stranger's life at a slight cost. However, if these minute-long intervals involved no such deprivations but only very mild pain that you would immediately forget, then it would not seem plausible that even a great total lifetime cost comprised entirely of *these* particular costs can yield a sufficiently strong permitting reason not to save another stranger's life at a slight cost.

This view of permitting reasons need not concern costs only. Fundamentally the view is that "lifetime" features can amplify permitting reasons present at the time of action, whether or not the lifetime features or permitting reasons are cost-based. For instance, considerations of autonomy can be incorporated in various ways: cost-based permitting reasons *or* autonomy-based permitting reasons not to save strangers may increase in strength as you incur a greater and greater lifetime cost *or* make a greater and greater difference to how your life unfolds in the course of saving more and more. Whether helping involves incurring costs or making a difference to how your life unfolds, you can sometimes permissibly refrain from saving strangers on the basis that you are doing enough already.

Since the view is about amplifying permitting reasons not to save strangers, it does not apply when there is no permitting reason to amplify in the first place. It is accordingly compatible with the plausible claim that, no matter how much lifetime cost you have incurred in saving strangers, you are required to save another stranger when doing so comes at no cost to you and makes no difference to how your life unfolds. Then the fact that you are doing enough already cannot make it permissible to refrain from helping.

The view (that permitting reasons not to save strangers increase in strength the greater the lifetime cost you incur in saving strangers) explains why in cases like *Frequent NearPlus* you are required to help on some occasions but not required to help on all occasions. Well before you help on all occasions, the lifetime cost you will have incurred yields a sufficiently strong permitting reason not to save another stranger, even if the cost of doing so is slight. The view achieves this in a way that is compatible with the plausible claim that there is a strong requiring reason to save each stranger you can.

However, so far the view provides only a partial solution to our problem about *Frequent NearPlus*. This is because it does not yet provide a plausible explanation of *when* you are required to help. According to a natural interpretation of the view, the permitting reason not to save a stranger is stronger, the greater the lifetime cost you have *already* incurred in saving strangers—here "doing enough already" is interpreted as "already done enough."

This interpretation of the view has the implication that, in *Frequent NearPlus*, you are required to save a stranger every time you can until you have incurred enough lifetime cost that there is a sufficiently strong permitting reason not to save another stranger. This interpretation effectively carves your life into a very demanding early period and a very permissive later period. If the early period is even just a few months, the "already done enough" interpretation has the seemingly overly demanding implication that you are required to do virtually nothing but save strangers for this period of your life (and notice that making the early period much shorter would make the later period even more permissive).

We can avoid the implication of an overly demanding early period if we adopt a different interpretation of the view that life-time features can amplify permitting reasons not to save strangers. Instead of claiming that the permitting reason not to save a stranger is stronger, the greater the lifetime cost you have *already* incurred, we can claim that this permitting reason is stronger, the greater the lifetime cost you reasonably expect you *will* have incurred.[4]

To be able to reasonably expect that you will have done enough, you typically will need to make genuine and well-founded plans to do enough, maintain your commitment to them over time (by somewhat regularly putting them into action), and update them in light of changes in your circumstances.[5] Over time your reasonable expectation of having done enough will wax and wane. Permitting reasons not to help will accordingly be amplified more or less by this lifetime feature. The result is that you can sometimes permissibly refrain from saving strangers on the basis that you will have done enough. You might even be so altruistic that at each time throughout your life you reasonably expect you will have done enough. Then at each time it would be permissible not to help. Even so, you could still be required to help some of the time *in the sense that*, if you do not help enough of the time, you would then at least occasionally be unable to reasonably expect that you will have done enough, and on those occasions you would be required to help.[6]

What if you reasonably expect that later in life you are going to be lazy and selfish? Then the "will've done enough" interpretation of the view could carve your life into a very demanding early period and a very permissive later period—since you're not going to do any stranger-saving later, you've got to do it all now. But this implication seems plausible. After all, the reason you've got to do it all now is that *you're not going to* take opportunities to help later. Just as you could end up with a more demanding later period of life if you refuse to help earlier, you could end up with a more demanding earlier period of life if you refuse to help later. If you refuse to help during any given period, well, that's up to you, but your permitting reasons won't be amplified as much.

Some may find it implausible that you could end up with a much more demanding earlier period if you refuse to help later. They could modify the view so that the permitting reasons present at the time of action are amplified not only as a function of (expected) costs incurred over your lifetime but also as a function of (expected) costs incurred closer to the time of action. This extra amplification could prevent selfishness and laziness during one period of your life from resulting in overdemandingness at other times. Even if you won't be doing enough over the course of your life, you might still be doing enough for the time being.[7] The view can be similarly modified to avoid periods of overpermissiveness. Perhaps when there is enough temporal or psychological distance between the time of action and the time the (expected) costs are incurred, amplification cannot turn an otherwise insufficiently strong permitting reason into a sufficiently strong permitting reason. Then we could claim that, even if you were a saint in your 20s, you cannot permissibly refuse to incur slight costs to save strangers all throughout your 50s.

In sum, the "will've done enough" interpretation of the view that lifetime features can amplify permitting reasons not to save strangers allows you to approach cases like *Frequent NearPlus* with a lifetime plan for saving strangers so that you can permissibly locate your stranger-saving earlier or later or spread it out in various ways. It captures a plausible sense in which beneficence is an "imperfect duty."[8] The main arguments in this book do not depend on deciding between the "already done enough" and "will've done enough" interpretations of the view that lifetime features can amplify permitting reasons not to incur costs in saving strangers. Nonetheless, as I have suggested, I favor the "will've done enough" interpretation. A full account of when and why you can permissibly refrain from helping in cases like *Frequent NearPlus* would include further details.[9] But any plausible account will centrally appeal to the presence of permitting reasons, rather than to the absence of requiring reasons. Any plausible account will accommodate the claim that there is an equally strong requiring reason to save each individual stranger.

6.4. Cost, Autonomy, and Switching Off

In the last section of the previous chapter, I looked at a case that is as rare as *Pond* but is like *Charity* with respect to distance, salience, uniqueness, injustice, and diffusion (*FarPlus*). And I compared it with an equally rare case that is like *Pond* with respect to distance, salience, uniqueness, injustice, and diffusion (*NearPlus*). We were to take these cases as occurring in an imaginary world in which your opportunities to help are very rare. In such a world, considerations of lifetime cost do little, if anything, to amplify permitting reasons not to help.

The real world, by contrast, contains both rare cases like *Pond* as well as very frequent cases like *Charity*. If considerations of lifetime cost can permit you not to save as many strangers as possible in *Frequent NearPlus*, then they can permit you not to donate in a very frequent case like *Charity*. Could they also permit you not to help in a rare case like *Pond*? Suppose that, because you have already or will have donated in several cases like *Charity*, considerations of lifetime cost yield a sufficiently strong permitting reason to take a break from donating your time and money. You permissibly "switch off" from charitable giving for a while, instead turning your attention to your own personal projects and plans. Unexpectedly, you find yourself in a rare case like *Pond*. It may seem that, while it is permissible not to donate $3000 to a malaria charity that saves on average one life for every donation of this size, it would be wrong not to save the drowning stranger even when saving them involves a monetary sacrifice of $3000 or more.

Can the fact that cases like *Charity* are very frequent while cases like *Pond* are very rare make it permissible not to help in *Charity* even when it would have been wrong not to help in *Pond*? To answer this question, we need to consider another properly controlled case.

Rare/Frequent NearPlus: You are in *Frequent NearPlus*, but in addition to indicating every minute that yet another boulder is threatening yet another stranger, your trusty phone will very rarely indicate that a small iron meteorite is threatening a lone stranger 10 feet away on the other side of a tall brick wall. As before, your phone will then display a live video of the stranger, and you will find it difficult to put their plight out of your mind. You will realize that you are able to save their life. If you stand on a red button for a minute, this will bring about a 99 percent chance that a large underground magnet—located a few miles away—will divert the meteorite into an empty field, saving the stranger. No one else can help the lone stranger. During the minute that you are able to save a stranger from a meteorite by standing on the red button, you will be unable to use your phone to save a stranger from a boulder. You cannot stand on both the red button and the green button at the same time—so you can't collect $3000 from the green button while you're on the red button. But if you do stand on the green button during the minute that you could have saved someone from a meteorite by standing on the red button, you cannot use the money obtained from the green button during that minute to later save a stranger from a boulder (during that minute, standing on the green button would get you $3000 in cash rather than the usual electronic money, and you can't use cash on your phone to save a stranger from a boulder). While you can switch off the very frequent boulder-emergency notifications on your phone, you cannot switch off the rare meteorite-emergency notifications.

In *Rare/Frequent NearPlus*, you face an indefinitely long series of opportunities to help of the following sort: . . . *Boulder, Boulder, Boulder, Boulder, Boulder,* **Meteorite***, Boulder, Boulder* . . . . These opportunities arise each minute. The cost of saving a stranger from a boulder is one minute of your time ($3000), the cost of saving a stranger from a meteorite is one minute of your time ($3000), and there is never a conflict between saving a stranger from a boulder and saving a stranger from a meteorite.[10]

Now suppose that, by saving several strangers from being crushed by boulders, you incur enough lifetime cost to yield a sufficiently strong permitting reason to take a break from saving. You permissibly switch off the boulder-emergency notifications on your phone for a while, instead turning your attention to your own personal projects and plans. Unexpectedly, you find yourself in a position to save a lone stranger from being crushed by a meteorite—your trusty phone grabs your attention, describes the emergency at hand, and makes the lone stranger's plight vivid to you. Are there circumstances in which, while it is permissible not to save a stranger from being crushed by a boulder, it would have been wrong not to save a lone stranger from a meteorite?

In *Rare/Frequent NearPlus*, opportunities to save strangers from boulders are very frequent, and opportunities to save strangers from meteorites are very rare. But this difference does not on its own explain how it could be permissible not to save a stranger from a boulder even when it would have been wrong not to save a lone stranger from a meteorite. By saving strangers from boulders, you incur a lifetime cost that amplifies permitting reasons not to *save strangers*—whether from boulders, meteorites, malaria, or what have you. The lifetime cost incurred in saving strangers from boulders doesn't exclusively amplify permitting reasons not to save strangers *from boulders*.[11]

Nonetheless, there are considerations correlated with frequency that can explain how it is *sometimes* permissible not to save a stranger from a boulder even when it would have been wrong not to save a lone stranger from a meteorite. It may at first appear that the cost of saving a stranger from a meteorite is equivalent to the cost of saving a stranger from a boulder. To save a stranger from a meteorite, you would have to incur a loss of one minute ($3000), and to save a stranger from a boulder, you would have to incur a loss of one minute ($3000). But once you have switched off boulder-emergency notifications, saving a stranger from a boulder sometimes involves incurring the *further costs* of switching back on your attention to these frequent opportunities to help.

Switching off from the frequent opportunities to save strangers from boulders enables you to enjoy psychological freedom from them and to attend to your personal projects and plans. In switching back on, you may incur the psychological burdens of attending to this ongoing situation of need, and you may interrupt your projects and plans. By contrast, rare opportunities to save strangers from meteorites arise unexpectedly, and are likely to hijack your attention and interrupt your plans. You'd *bear* these costs but not *incur* them; they'd result from bad luck rather than your choice. But in saving someone from a boulder once you have switched off, you would incur the costs of switching back on. You would impose these costs on yourself.[12]

In short, once you've switched off boulder-emergency notifications, the cost you would have to incur to save a stranger from a boulder is sometimes significantly greater than the cost you would have to incur to save a stranger from a meteorite. Sometimes, to save a stranger from a boulder you would have to incur *both* the loss of one minute ($3000) *and* the significant costs of switching back on. To save a stranger from a meteorite, you would have to incur only the former cost.

In addition, since whether you switch back on to a frequently occurring opportunity to help may make a significant difference to how your life unfolds, there may also be a significant *autonomy*-based permitting reason not to switch back on. By contrast, you are typically unable to switch off from rare opportunities in the first place (hence the stipulation in *Rare/Frequent NearPlus* that you are unable to switch off meteorite-emergency notifications). Being confronted with a rare opportunity to help may of course make a significant difference to how your life unfolds, but autonomy-based permitting reasons depend on the existence of alternatives, where *your choice* between them would make a significant difference to how your life unfolds.

These cost-based and autonomy-based differences between frequent opportunities and rare opportunities can get amplified. Consider costs. The cost of one minute does not itself yield a sufficiently strong permitting reason not to save a stranger from a meteorite, and even if the cost of one minute together with the cost of switching back on yields a significantly stronger permitting reason not to save a stranger from a boulder, it may also fail to be sufficiently strong. But a small difference in the strength of these permitting reasons can become a large difference when amplified by lifetime features. Such amplification can give us a range of cases in which, while it is permissible not to save a stranger from a boulder, it would have been wrong not to save a stranger from a meteorite.

Here is an illustrative model. Suppose that when you incur a given lifetime cost in the course of helping strangers, this amplifies to degree L the permitting reasons not to incur further costs. Saving a stranger from a meteorite comes at cost C. Saving a stranger from a boulder (once you've switched off from boulder-emergency notifications) comes at significantly greater cost $C+$. The difference in strength of the permitting reasons not to incur these costs corresponds to the difference between C and $C+$. But the difference in strength of these permitting reasons amplified by lifetime features corresponds to the difference between $[L \times C]$ and $[L \times C+]$. Even when the permitting reasons corresponding to C and $C+$ are not strong enough to prevent the balance of requiring reasons from making it wrong not to save a stranger, the permitting reasons corresponding to $[L \times C]$ and $[L \times C+]$ may be strong enough to do so. And, for a range of lifetime costs, the permitting reason corresponding to $[L \times C]$ is not strong enough to prevent the balance of requiring reasons from making it wrong not to save a stranger from a meteorite, but the permitting reason corresponding to $[L \times C+]$ is strong enough to prevent the balance of requiring reasons from making it wrong not to save a stranger from a boulder.[13] So, there is a range of cases in which, while it is permissible not to save a stranger from a boulder, it would have been wrong not to save a stranger from a meteorite. Further note that even if the cost of saving a stranger from a meteorite is *two* minutes ($6000), sometimes the cost of one minute ($3000) together with the costs of switching back on is greater. As the model shows, there'd still be a range of cases in which, while it is permissible not to save a stranger from a boulder, it would have been wrong not to save a stranger from a meteorite. The amplification of autonomy-based differences between frequent opportunities and rare opportunities can have similar effects.

6.5. Implications for Ponds and Charities

Rare/Frequent NearPlus shows how there can be cost-based and autonomy-based permitting reasons not to switch back on to frequently occurring opportunities to help. This has implications for cases like *Pond*, *Charity*, and *Pond v. Charity*.

In exploring these implications, I set aside risky diffusion. After all, if *Pond* is like *Concentration* with respect to risky diffusion and *Charity* is like *Risky Diffusion* with respect to risky diffusion, this could plausibly explain why it is sometimes permissible not to donate in cases like *Charity* yet wrong not to help in cases like *Pond* (and why it is permissible or even required to save the drowning stranger in cases like *Pond v. Charity*). In setting aside risky diffusion, we rule out this explanation. For the remainder of this chapter, I assume that *Pond* is like *NearPlus* with respect to distance, salience, uniqueness, injustice, and open diffusion, whereas *Charity* is like *FarPlus* with respect to these same factors. Of course, *Pond* and *Charity* take place in a world in which cases like *Charity* occur very frequently, whereas *NearPlus* and *FarPlus* take place in an imaginary world in which all opportunities to help strangers are very rare. The crucial point here is that, given the above assumption, risky diffusion cannot explain why it is sometimes permissible not to donate in cases like *Charity* yet wrong not to help in cases like *Pond* (or why it is sometimes permissible to save the drowning stranger in cases like *Pond v. Charity*). Nonetheless, permitting reasons correlated with frequency can explain this. Or so I now argue.

In the real world, you can anticipate when frequent *Charity*-like cases will occur (all the time) but not when rare *Pond*-like cases will occur. Suppose that, while you can switch off from *Charity*-like cases, you cannot switch off from *Pond*-like cases. When you are in a *Charity*-like case, you are able to attend to your personal projects and plans instead of the distant strangers you could help by donating. But when in a *Pond*-like case, the drowning stranger has your attention so that you are at least momentarily unable to attend to your personal projects and plans. Now suppose you switch off from charitable giving for a while, enjoying some degree of psychological freedom from it and attending to your own personal projects and plans. Unexpectedly, you find yourself in a rare *Pond*-like case.

Suppose that in this *Pond*-like case you would lose $3000 in the course of saving the drowning stranger, and further suppose that this money cannot instead be used to donate in a *Charity*-like case. You face an indefinitely long series of opportunities to help of the following sort: . . . *Charity, Charity, Charity, Charity, Charity, Charity,* **Pond***, Charity, Charity* . . . . There is never a conflict between donating to charity and saving a drowning stranger. Given the clear similarities to *Rare/Frequent NearPlus*, we can draw a similar conclusion: there are permitting reasons not to switch back on to charitable giving that, when amplified by lifetime features, yield a range of cases in which it is permissible not to donate $3000 in a *Charity*-like case, even though it would have been wrong not to help in a *Pond*-like case at an equal monetary cost.

Next suppose that the monetary cost of saving the drowning stranger is $6000. As before, there'd still be a range of cases in which it is permissible not to donate $3000 in a *Charity*-like case, even though it would have been wrong not to save the drowning stranger at this greater monetary cost.

Things are importantly different if we suppose, more realistically, that the $6000 you would lose in the course of saving the drowning stranger *can* instead be used to donate in a *Charity*-like case. Now there is sometimes a conflict between donating to charity and saving a drowning stranger. You face an indefinitely long series of opportunities to help of the following sort: . . . *Charity, Charity, Charity, Charity, Charity,* **Pond v. Charity***, Charity, Charity* . . . .

Permitting reasons not to switch back on to charitable giving can (together with lifetime features) make it permissible to save the drowning stranger in a significant range of cases like *Pond v. Charity*. Suppose you switch off from charitable giving for a while, enjoying some degree of psychological freedom from it and attending to your own personal projects and plans. Unexpectedly, you find yourself in a case like *Pond v. Charity*. Sometimes the cost you would have to incur to save the greater number by letting the stranger drown and donating the $6000 to the malaria charity is significantly greater than the cost you would have to incur to save the drowning stranger. Sometimes, to save the greater number by donating to the malaria charity you would have to incur *both* the monetary loss of $6000 *and* the significant cost of switching back on to charitable giving. Although your projects and plans would have already been interrupted by the drowning stranger, you may still incur psychological costs in switching back on to charitable giving. There is a practically endless series of distant strangers you could help by giving to charity but only one drowning stranger. At least when you're switched off from charitable giving, saving the one stranger from drowning can provide a sense of having "completely dealt with the problem."[14]

In addition, since whether you save a drowning stranger or let them die so that you can donate to charity may make a significant difference to how your life unfolds, there may also be a significant autonomy-based permitting reason to take either of these alternatives. This sort of permitting reason could persist even if switching back on to charitable giving were not costly to you. It could also persist in cases in which you have not switched off from charitable giving.

These cost-based and autonomy-based permitting reasons may not be enough on their own to make it permissible to save the drowning stranger rather than donate the $6000 to the malaria charity. However, when sufficiently amplified by lifetime features, either can make it permissible to save the drowning stranger.

Given the assumption made earlier that *Pond* is like *NearPlus* with respect to distance, salience, uniqueness, injustice, and open diffusion, whereas *Charity* is like *FarPlus* with respect to these same factors, it is plausible that in *Pond v. Charity* there is most requiring reason overall to let the stranger drown and donate to the malaria charity (there is most requiring reason overall to save the greater number in *NearPlus v. FarPlus*). So, even when it is permissible to save the drowning stranger—thanks to a sufficiently strong permitting reason—it also remains permissible to let the stranger drown and donate to the malaria charity.

In fact, it can happen that there is no sufficiently strong permitting reason to do nothing even though there is a sufficiently strong permitting reason to save the drowning stranger rather than donate (suppose the monetary cost of helping in either way is relatively small, but the cost of switching back on to charitable giving is relatively large). In such a case, it is wrong to do nothing, permissible to save the drowning stranger, and permissible to donate the money to the malaria charity. You are required to help in one way or the other but neither in particular.[15]

What about the range of cases in which there is no sufficiently strong permitting reason to save the drowning stranger rather than donate? We may be reluctant to accept the implication that it is *wrong* to save the drowning stranger. But then the fact that it seems wrong to save the one in *NearPlus v. FarPlus* would suggest we are not properly taking on board the assumption that *Pond* is like *NearPlus* with respect to distance, salience, uniqueness, injustice, and open diffusion, whereas *Charity* is like *FarPlus* with respect to these same factors.[16] When this assumption is properly taken on board and when it is clear that there is no sufficiently strong permitting reason to save the drowning stranger in *Pond v. Charity*, it seems wrong to save the drowning stranger.

Others may object that, even when there is a sufficiently strong permitting reason to save the drowning stranger, permissibility does not go far enough. According to them, you're *required* to save the drowning stranger. But I do not see why this should be so, unless we drop the above assumption (notice that you're not required to save the lesser number in *NearPlus v. FarPlus*; in this case, there is most requiring reason overall to save the greater number). If we do drop this assumption, we could then argue that, since *Pond v. Charity* is like *Concentration v. Risky Diffusion* with respect to risky diffusion, you are required to save the drowning stranger rather than donate. My aim here has been to see how far we can get without appealing to risky diffusion. We seem to be near the limit.[17]

Notes

1. For discussion of similar cases, see Cullity 2004, Sin 2010, Woollard 2015, Timmerman 2015, and Thomson 2021.
2. On cutoffs and vagueness in ethics, see Ellis 1992, Dougherty 2014, Schoenfield 2016, Pummer 2022, and Pummer forthcoming.
3. The requiring reason to save enough strangers can be thought of as an *imperfect* requiring reason in that it leaves it open when to help, as long as you help enough of the time. As argued below in this section, we should reject all views that imply that there are no requiring reasons to save any of the individual strangers in cases like *Frequent NearPlus*. Nonetheless, as argued further below (in section 6.3), there is a view that implies that there are requiring reasons to save each and every individual stranger yet

still effectively treats the duty to help strangers as an imperfect duty. We should prefer this view. (In some cases there's only a requiring reason to perform enough acts out of a set of possible acts and no requiring reasons to perform any of these individual acts. For instance, suppose that if you stand on a button for any two minutes over the next hour, a stranger will be saved. There's only a requiring reason to stand on the button for enough minutes over the next hour and no requiring reasons to stand on the button for any of the individual minutes that make up the next hour.)

4. Alternatively, we could claim that the permitting reason not to save a stranger is stronger, the greater the cost you have already incurred and the greater the cost you *in fact* can (or will) incur. Such an alternative view makes the permissibility of not helping now independent of your present expectation of having done enough. The view discussed in the main text is more suitable for subjective (or evidence-relative) permissibility. At least, I take it that having the reasonable expectation that you are not going to help later would compel you to help now, were you morally decent. For relevant literature, see Portmore 2019, Timmerman 2019, Sebo and Paul 2019, Timmerman and Cohen 2020, White 2021, and Pummer unpublished.

5. You could also take a pledge. See, for example, https://www.givingwhatwecan.org/.

6. In this way my view implies that whether it is permissible not to help can depend on whether you will help enough. Further related issues arise in variants of *Frequent NearPlus* in which the cost of helping on each occasion in the future depends on whether you help now. For example, suppose that if you do not help now, the cost of helping on each occasion in the future will be *very* slight so that you can reasonably expect that if you do not help now you will not have incurred enough lifetime cost in helping others, making it wrong not to help now. And suppose that, if you do help now, the cost of helping on each occasion in the future will be moderate so that you can reasonably expect that independently of helping now you will have done enough, making it permissible not to help now. One response is that you ought to help now, since it's permissible to help now if you help now, whereas it's wrong not to help now if you

don't help now. For discussion of normative variance, see Bykvist 2007 and Spencer 2021.

7. Compare with Smith 1990 (25) and Woollard 2015 (131–133) on "ongoing sacrifice."

8. Unlike standard views according to which beneficence is an imperfect duty, my view maintains that there are ("perfect") requiring reasons to help each and every stranger you can. On my view, the duty to help is imperfect thanks to permitting reasons *not* to help more than enough of the time. This way of arriving at imperfect duties has gone largely unnoticed. It is briefly considered by Hanser 2014, who writes: "On this alternative account, first-order requiring reasons (which would ordinarily constitute perfect duties) are transformed into imperfect duties by the existence of a second-order permission to ignore such duties from time to time" (311). But he is skeptical: "why should it be morally permissible sometimes (perhaps often) to ignore *duties* of a certain kind? Wouldn't this tend to undermine the idea that they really are duties?" (312). The framework I have offered here provides an explanation. There are requiring reasons (which absent countervailing considerations would constitute perfect duties) to save strangers. This is seen in various rescue cases of the sort discussed in Chapter 5, taken as occurring in an imaginary world in which your opportunities to help are very rare. But when there is a sufficiently strong permitting reason not to help, these requiring reasons to help do not *require* you to do so. The great cost to you of helping can be a sufficiently strong permitting reason not to help. Likewise, in realistic worlds in which your opportunities to help are very frequent, there can be a sufficiently strong permitting reason not to incur costs in helping others, based on the fact that you reasonably expect you will have done enough. Requiring reasons can thus sometimes be permissibly ignored. Of course, when you reasonably expect that you will not have done enough, you cannot permissibly ignore them. For some of the literature on imperfect duties of beneficence, see Hill 2002, Timmermann 2005, Noggle 2009, Greenspan 2010, Herman 2012, Hanser 2014, and Portmore 2019. For relevant discussion of beneficence over time, see Dougherty 2017 and Cordelli 2018.

9. I provide some such details in Pummer unpublished.

10. The cost of *paying* $3000 to save a stranger from a boulder seems relevantly similar to the cost of *not collecting* $3000 to save a stranger from a meteorite, given that you can collect another $3000 each minute you stand on the green button.

11. Also see Woollard's 2015 (126–127) reply to Schmidtz 2000, showing his reply to Unger 1996 to be unsuccessful.

12. To further appreciate the significance of *incurring* costs as opposed to merely bearing them, suppose a stranger's life will be saved if and only if you die at 5 p.m. It is plausible that you are not required to bring it about that you die at 5 p.m., given that you would otherwise live many good years. But now consider a variant of the case in which a brain aneurysm is due to kill you at 5:01 p.m. Now it is plausible that you are required to bring it about that you die at 5 p.m. Even if in each case you suffer the same great cost, you impose this great cost on yourself only in the first case. In the second case, you impose only a tiny fraction of the cost on yourself. I do not deny that the costs you merely bear can be relevant to the strength of permitting reasons not to incur costs. But costs that are incurred seem to be of particular significance to the strength of permitting reasons not to incur further costs.

13. We can think of this as a model of "golden opportunities" to help (Noggle 2009), where an opportunity to help is more golden to the extent that the permitting reasons not to take it are weaker than usual or the requiring reasons to take it are stronger than usual. Sometimes you are permitted to switch off from usual opportunities but would nonetheless be required to respond to relevantly unusual ones.

14. Contrary to Unger 1996 (41), this sense of completion is justifiable— when it is permissible to switch off from the "continuing mess in the world," you don't have to regard the plight of the drowning stranger as part of this mess. Contrary to Kamm 2007 (363), the justifiability of this sense of completion does not depend on distance having moral significance.

15. Kamm 2000 (677–681) arrives at these verdicts via a different route. She argues that, while a duty to rescue the drowning stranger makes it wrong to do nothing, you can permissibly "substitute" donating for rescuing the stranger, even when you do not have a duty to donate. Also see Woollard 2015 (155–156).

16. Another possibility is that intuitions about *Pond v. Charity* are affected by uncertainty about whether, if you do not save the drowning stranger, you *will* in fact go on to donate the $6000 rather than spend it on luxuries. We can make *Pond v. Charity* even more like *NearPlus v. FarPlus* by imagining that, within the next few seconds, you can either rush into the pond or deposit the $6000 into a cash machine that directly transfers the money to the malaria charity (there's not enough time to do both).

17. The intuition had by some that it is wrong to donate rather than save the drowning stranger in cases like *Pond v. Charity* may be due to suspicions about your motivations for donating. It is unusual for anyone to be so strongly moved to save distant strangers through donating to charity that they would let someone drown right before their eyes. Some may accordingly suspect that, if you donate rather than save the drowning stranger, you must have had some ulterior motive or been inadequately moved by the plight of the drowning stranger. But even if you were blameworthy for donating from some bad motivation, that doesn't imply that it is wrong to donate (and it seems to me you would not be blameworthy for donating rather than saving the drowning stranger if you were adequately moved by the plight of the drowning stranger but moved *more* by the plights of the distant many). For further discussion, see Woollard 2015 (156), Chappell 2019, and Mogensen 2019.

7 | SPECIAL CONNECTIONS

7.1. Does Charity Begin at Home?

In the previous two chapters, I looked at *Pond* and *Charity*, exploring which differences between them, if any, could make it permissible not to help in cases like *Charity* even when it would be wrong not to help at a similar cost in cases like *Pond*. I also explored which such differences, if any, could make it at least permissible to save fewer rather than more strangers in cases like *Pond v. Charity*. In Chapter 5, I focused on differences with respect to distance, salience, uniqueness, injustice, and diffusion. Apart from a type of diffusion ("risky diffusion"), I argued that these factors do not make the relevant sort of moral difference. In Chapter 6, I discussed differences with respect to frequency. I developed a view according to which lifetime features can amplify permitting reasons not to save strangers so that how much you will have done over the course of your life can make it permissible not to incur (even slight) costs in saving more strangers. In this way, it can matter whether you find yourself in a world in which opportunities to help strangers at cost are very frequent or very rare. The relative

The Rules of Rescue. Theron Pummer, Oxford University Press. © Oxford University Press 2023.
DOI: 10.1093/oso/9780190884147.003.0008

frequency of specific types of opportunities to help does not itself make a difference to requiring reasons or permitting reasons. It doesn't itself matter whether you save someone from a humdrum boulder or an improbable meteorite. Nonetheless, considerations correlated with frequency, like the cost of "switching back on," can make a significant difference to permitting reasons.

There is a further difference between cases like *Pond* and cases like *Charity* (and within cases like *Pond v. Charity*) that I have so far bracketed: typically, in cases like *Pond* those you can help are members of your own community, whereas in cases like *Charity* they are not. In the clean cases discussed in the previous two chapters, the strangers you can rescue are not members of your community. The fact that there are strong requiring reasons to help in all these cases shows that charity at least doesn't *end* at home. We may still wonder whether charity nonetheless begins at home, in the sense that there are stronger reasons to help those who are members of your own community—village, town, city, region, or country—than there are to help those who are not. Depending on the community in question, members of your community are more likely to be your friends, relatives, colleagues, associates, acquaintances, and so on. What is the moral significance of these sorts of *special connections*? (Being members of the same community may constitute its own special connection, independently of being friends, relatives, colleagues, and so on.) The focus of this chapter is whether, when, and how special connections affect requiring reasons or permitting reasons to save others.[1]

In section 7.2, I look at some of the ways in which reasons can be enhanced by special connections, in accord with the kinds and degrees of these connections. In section 7.3, I show how lifetime features can amplify otherwise insufficiently strong (permitting and requiring) reasons to save a lesser number of people to whom you are specially connected over a greater number of strangers, making it permissible or even required to save the lesser number. In section 7.4, I show how responsibly acquired special connections can increase the cost you are required to incur in helping others over the course of your life.

7.2. Kinds and Degrees of Connections

In this section, I look at some of the different ways in which reasons can be enhanced by special connections, in accord with the kinds and degrees of these connections. I temporarily set aside complications of frequency and the corresponding amplifying effects of lifetime features. It can therefore be useful to again suppose that the cases discussed in this section take place in an imaginary world in which your opportunities to help are very rare.

Consider the following cases.

Friend: While out for a hike in a country you have never been to before, you see on the map of your phone a red dot indicating that there is an emergency about 1000 miles away from you. You tap the dot for a brief description of the situation. It turns out that, on the other side of a tall brick wall, a boulder is hurtling toward your *friend*, *A*, who is stuck in the boulder's path. You cannot reach *A* yourself but realize that, for $X, you can save *A*'s life using your phone. Many other people can similarly help A, but you are certain none of them will. As it happens, you would never see A again anyway as they're about to move to a remote monastery where they would stay for the rest of their life. Also, you recently accidentally ingested an antidepressant that would make the psychological costs of letting a friend (like A) die roughly equivalent to the psychological costs of letting a stranger die.

Stranger: While out for a hike in a country you have never been to before, you see on the map of your phone a red dot indicating that there is an emergency about 1000 miles away from you. It turns out that, on the other side of a tall brick wall, a boulder is hurtling toward a *stranger*, B. The remaining details are just like those in *Friend*.

A friend's death would typically be much costlier to you than a stranger's—both psychologically and in terms of missing out on good times you would otherwise have had with your friend. Such cost differences are controlled for in *Friend*. Even so, it seems plausible that, at least if your special connection to A is of an adequate kind and degree, you can be required to pay $X to help in *Friend* yet permitted not to pay this amount (or similar) to help in *Stranger*.

Similarly, in *Friend v. Strangers* (the details of which the reader can fill in), it seems plausible that, at least if your special connection to A is of an adequate kind and degree, it is permissible to pay $X to save your friend, A, instead of paying $X to save two strangers. It may even be wrong to save the two strangers instead of saving A.

There are various *kinds* of special connections. Personal relationships such as those of friends, relatives, and colleagues are paradigm cases of special connections. You can also have a special connection to someone through a project or commitment without having a personal relationship with them. Consider a volunteer who has a project of helping cancer victims, whomever they may be. Some kinds of special connections enhance requiring reasons, whereas others enhance permitting reasons.[2] For instance, it is plausible that, while parenthood and promises enhance requiring reasons, personal projects enhance permitting reasons. Sufficiently immoral connections—such as those between Nazis—do not enhance either sort of reason.

Special connections come in various *degrees*. Close friends and relatives have the most special of personal relationships. Connections get progressively less special as we move from close friends and relatives to not-so-close friends and relatives to mere acquaintances to strangers you've only just met to strangers you've never met. Connections similarly get progressively less special as we move from central life projects and commitments to not-so-central "side" projects to fleeting desires and whims. Special connections enhance reasons less, the less special they are.

If in *Friend v. Strangers* your special connection to *A* is sufficiently special—if *A* is a reasonably close friend—then it seems at least permissible to save *A* instead of the two strangers. Whether it is wrong to save the two strangers depends on whether friendship is the sort of special connection that enhances requiring reasons or permitting reasons. If it sufficiently enhances the requiring reason to save *A*, then it is wrong to save the two strangers. It could likewise be wrong to save one stranger's life instead of saving *A*'s legs.

What if *A* were instead a mere acquaintance? Suppose you have seen *A* hiking a few times while you were riding your bike to work, and on two occasions you exchanged greetings and smiles. It seems this sort of connection would not sufficiently enhance either the requiring reason or the permitting reason to save *A*. It would remain wrong to save *A*, given that you could have instead saved two non-acquaintances at the same cost to yourself. Perhaps your mild acquaintanceship with *A* could nonetheless make it permissible to save *A* from a headache instead of saving two non-acquaintances from equally bad headaches, when it would otherwise be wrong to do so.

What if *A* weren't even an acquaintance but a mere compatriot (citizen of the same country as you)? At least insofar as you are a civilian who lacks any special role-based responsibility to prioritize the lives of compatriots over the lives of non-compatriots, it does not seem permissible to save *A*'s life when you could at the same cost to yourself save the lives of two non-compatriots instead. Even if compatriotism is morally significant, it does not make a sufficient moral difference in cases like *Friend v. Strangers* in which *A* is a mere compatriot.[3]

At the beginning of this chapter, I noted that there can be differences with respect to special connections between cases like *Pond* and cases like *Charity* and within cases like *Pond v. Charity*. In addition, "*Pond v. Pond*" and "*Charity v. Charity*" cases can likewise differ with respect to special connections. Consider the following case in which you can donate to a charity to which you have a special connection or donate the same amount to a more cost-effective charity to which you have no special connection.

Cancer v. Malaria: Over the course of your whole life, you will have only one opportunity to help others. When this opportunity arises, you can help in only one of two ways. You can either donate $X to a cancer charity that on average saves one life per $X donated or instead donate $X to a malaria charity that on average saves two lives per $X donated. When you lost a parent to cancer a few years ago, you acquired the central life project of helping cancer victims. You have really wanted to advance this project, but you have not yet had a chance to do so. Now is your only chance. Also, you recently accidentally ingested an antidepressant that makes the psychological costs of not donating to the cancer charity roughly equivalent to the psychological costs of not donating to the malaria charity.

It seems plausible that your special connection to the cancer charity could in such a case make it permissible to donate $X to the cancer charity instead of donating $X to the malaria charity, even though the latter saves on average twice as many lives per dollar donated. (I tend to think projects can give rise to permitting reasons independently of costs, but others may hold that the permitting reasons to which projects give rise are ultimately cost-based. They can transpose my arguments accordingly.)

Cases like *Charity*, *Pond v. Charity*, and *Cancer v. Malaria* involve a potential complication: risky diffusion. In Chapter 5, I claimed that *Pond v. Charity* may be like *Concentration v. Risky Diffusion* with respect to risky diffusion and that this is plausibly morally significant. For example, it may be permissible to pay $X to save one stranger for sure instead of paying $X to bring about a 1/300 chance that 600 other strangers are saved (even though the latter has twice the expected value in terms of lives saved). Similarly, it may be that the degree to which *there is more requiring reason overall to save two strangers for sure than there is to save one other stranger for sure* is greater than the degree to which *there is more requiring reason overall to bring about a 1/300 chance that 600 strangers are saved than there is to bring about a 1/300 chance that 300 other strangers are saved*. If so, then it would take more to overturn the balance of requiring reasons in the former "certainty" case than in the latter "risky diffusion" case.

It seems plausible that your project of helping cancer victims in *Cancer v. Malaria* is a special enough connection to the cancer charity to make it permissible to donate $X to the cancer charity rather than donate $X to the malaria charity, where this involves bringing about a 1/300 chance that 300 cancer deaths are prevented rather than bringing about a 1/300 chance that 600 malaria deaths are prevented. But perhaps this connection isn't special enough to make it permissible to save one from cancer for sure rather than save two from malaria for sure. At any rate, connections of mere acquaintanceship and mere compatriotism are less special still. Even if it were permissible to cure the headaches of 300 acquaintances (or compatriots) instead of curing the headaches of 600 others, it doesn't seem permissible to bring about a 1/300 chance that the lives of 300 acquaintances (or compatriots) are saved instead of bringing about a 1/300 chance that the lives of 600 others are saved. It seems to me these sorts of connections cannot plausibly make it permissible to produce half the expected value in terms of lives saved.[4]

7.3. Lifetime Features and Special Connections

Special connections can enhance requiring reasons or permitting reasons to save others, even in imaginary worlds in which your opportunities to help are very rare. As argued in Chapter 6, various lifetime features come into play in more realistic worlds in which your opportunities to help are frequent. In this section, I show how lifetime features can amplify otherwise insufficiently strong (permitting and requiring) reasons to save a lesser number of people to whom you are specially connected over a greater number of strangers, making it permissible or even required to save the lesser number. I show this using the following mashup of *Frequent NearPlus* and *Friend v. Strangers*.

> *Frequent Friend v. Strangers*: Once every minute for the indefinite future, you will be able to pay $3000 to save a different stranger from being crushed by a boulder. For the rest of your life, you will receive $3000 for every minute you stand on a large green button. This is the only way you can acquire money. There are no other ways of helping strangers—for example, you cannot ever donate to charities. Apart from taking breaks to do what you must in order to survive, you could spend the remainder of your life saving strangers from being crushed by boulders. You would not enjoy standing on the green button all day long, day after day. And, while standing on the green button, you would be incrementally missing out on things that make life worth living. *In addition*, on some number of occasions you will have the opportunity to pay $6000 to save a friend from being crushed by a boulder. (If there is more than one such occasion, it'll be

a different friend each time; I assume you could in theory have very many friends.)

First, I consider what happens if the special connections you have to your friends enhance the permitting reasons to save them without also enhancing the requiring reasons to save them. Then I turn to what happens if they enhance requiring reasons. (Throughout this section and the next I use "friends" for the sake of concreteness—the discussion also applies to other special connections beyond friendship.)

So, first, suppose that in *Frequent Friend v. Strangers* the special connections you have to your friends enhance the *permitting* reasons to save them without also enhancing the requiring reasons to save them. Suppose that there are equally strong reasons to save each friend.

If in *Frequent Friend v. Strangers*, the permitting reasons to save friends are strong enough to permit you to save any one friend instead of saving any two strangers, then you are permitted to spend $6000 to save one friend (instead of saving two strangers at $3000 each) *whenever* you can do so. And if there are sufficiently many such opportunities to save friends, you are permitted to spend all your money and time saving them, even if you could have instead saved twice as many strangers.

What if in *Frequent Friend v. Strangers* the permitting reasons to save friends were not strong enough to permit you to save any one friend instead of saving any two strangers? Even if so, it wouldn't follow that you are on no occasion permitted to spend $6000 to save one friend instead of saving two strangers at $3000 each. Recall from the previous chapter that costs incurred over the course of your life can amplify the permitting reason not to incur a cost on a given occasion. It is plausible that *forgoing saving friends* over the course of your life can likewise amplify the permitting reason not to forgo saving a friend on a given occasion—that is, it can amplify the permitting reason to save a friend.[5] In this way, lifetime features can amplify an otherwise insufficiently strong permitting reason to save a friend over two strangers. Assuming there are sufficiently many opportunities to save friends, it could thus turn out that on at least one occasion it is permissible to spend $6000 to save one friend instead of saving two strangers at $3000 each.

Next suppose that in *Frequent Friend v. Strangers* the special connections you have to your friends enhance the *requiring* reasons to save them. Suppose again that there are equally strong reasons to save each friend.

If in *Frequent Friend v. Strangers* the requiring reasons to save friends are strong enough to require you to save any one friend instead of saving any two strangers, then it is wrong to spend $6000 to save two strangers whenever you could have used it to save one friend instead. When you are not required to incur this cost to save a friend, we have another case in which it is wrong to save some and yet permissible to save none. But in this case, it is wrong to save the greater number, and you are conditionally required to save the lesser number. That is, you are required to (save a friend, given that you are going to spend $6000 to save anyone). (See Chapter 3 on conditional requirements.)

What if in *Frequent Friend v. Strangers* the requiring reasons to save friends were not strong enough to require you to save any one friend instead of saving any two strangers? Even if so, it wouldn't follow that you are on no occasion required to spend $6000 to save one friend instead of saving two strangers at $3000 each. Just as lifetime features can amplify permitting reasons, so too can they amplify requiring reasons. In particular, it is plausible that forgoing saving friends over the course of your life can amplify the requiring reason not to forgo saving a friend on a given occasion—that is, it can amplify the requiring reason to save a friend. In this way, lifetime features can amplify an otherwise insufficiently strong requiring reason to save a friend over two strangers. Assuming there are sufficiently many opportunities to save friends, it could thus turn out that on at least one occasion it is wrong to spend $6000 to save two strangers when you could have used it to save one friend instead. One way to think of it is that you can ignore weak requiring reasons to prioritize friends only so much. As you continually fail to respond to these reasons, they increase in strength, requiring you to on at least some occasions put your friends first.[6]

In sum, when faced with sufficiently many opportunities to save either one friend or two strangers, it can turn out that, even when the permitting or requiring reasons to save friends would otherwise be insufficiently strong, lifetime features can amplify them. They can do so to the point that on at least some occasions it is permissible to save a friend over two strangers or even wrong to save two strangers over a friend.

7.4. Lifetime Requirements

Do special connections affect the cost you can be required to incur in helping others over the course of your life? To get something of a baseline, first consider cases like *Frequent NearPlus*, in which the only others you can help are strangers to whom you have no special connections. How much cost are you required to incur over the course of your life in saving strangers in such a case? There are several factors relevant here. They include the costs of saving strangers, the lifetime well-being you would be left with as a result of saving them, the relative strength of the requiring reasons to help and the permitting reasons not to, and whether a multiplier view or an absolute limit view is correct. I cannot say with confidence how much cost you are required to incur over the course of your life in saving strangers in *Frequent NearPlus*. And there may be no precise answer. Still, keeping in mind that it isn't time or money but well-being and autonomy that are the bases of permitting reasons, it seems that, if you are roughly as well off as a typical member of an affluent country, you are required to give significantly more than 1 percent of your time and money but not required to give as much as 50 percent. For simplicity, let's go with *tithing*—let's assume that in *Frequent NearPlus* you are required to spend at least 10 percent of your time and money on saving strangers. With this in place, consider a new case.

Frequent Stranger v. Strangers: Once every minute for the indefinite future, you will be able to pay $3000 to save a different stranger from being crushed by a boulder. For the rest of your life, you will receive $3000 for every minute you stand on a large green button. This is the only way you can acquire money. There are no other ways of helping strangers—for example, you cannot ever donate to charities. Apart from taking breaks to do what you must in order to survive, you could spend the remainder of your life saving strangers from being crushed by boulders. You would not enjoy standing on the green button all day long, day after day. And, while standing on the green button, you would be incrementally missing out on things that make life worth living. *In addition*, on some number of occasions you will have the opportunity to pay $6000 to save a different stranger from being crushed by a boulder. That is, on these occasions, you have to decide whether to spend $6000 saving one *stranger* or saving two other *strangers* at $3000 each.

Given that in *Frequent NearPlus* you would save N strangers over the course of your life if you did the minimum required of spending 10 percent, it seems that in *Frequent Stranger v. Strangers* you are also required to save at least N strangers at a cost of at least 10 percent. Nonetheless, it would be wrong to incur a cost of 20 percent of your time and money to save N strangers at a cost of $6000 each. After all, you could have saved $2N$ strangers at no greater cost to yourself. There is more requiring reason overall to save $2N$ strangers than there is to save N strangers and no sufficiently strong permitting reason to save N strangers at the same cost. (And recall from Chapter 1 that there is no significant autonomy-based permitting reason to save N strangers rather than save $2N$ other strangers when this difference in which group is saved is the only significant difference between these alternatives.) Not only is it wrong to save a stranger at a cost of $6000 every time you help, but it is also wrong to do so on *any* occasion. On any such occasion, you could have saved two others at the same cost to yourself.

So, it is not plausible that, if in *Frequent Stranger v. Strangers* you are required to save at least N strangers at a cost to yourself of at least 10 percent of your time and money, then you are permitted to save N strangers at a cost to yourself of at least 10 percent of your time and money *by saving strangers at a cost of $6000 each.* As further evidence that this sort of inference fails, consider a variant of *Costly Conflict*: you can do nothing, save one stranger's life at the cost of stubbing your toe, save another stranger's life at the cost of losing your legs, or save two other strangers' lives at the cost of losing your legs. Although you are required to save at least one stranger's life at a cost of at least a stubbed toe, it is wrong to save one stranger's life at the cost of lost legs. After all, you could have saved two others at the same cost to yourself.

To get a baseline lifetime requirement, I have focused on strangers. How might introducing special connections affect the lifetime cost you can be required to incur in helping others? ("Others" are simply those who are not you, whether or not you have a special connection to them.)

It seems to matter whether special connections are *responsibly acquired.* To a first approximation, I take it that a special connection is responsibly acquired when you aren't coerced into acquiring it and you are relevantly aware of the implications of acquiring the connection (including the implications for what costs you could be required to incur). Your special connection to a friend or family member may be non-responsibly acquired to the extent that they end up needing your help in ways that you could not have reasonably expected. Indeed, most, if not all, real-world special connections are only *partially* responsibly acquired—we are virtually never relevantly aware of all the implications of acquiring a connection. There is much more discussion to be had about how this works in practice, but I take it that the responsibility condition would imply that many friendships and family relationships are to a significant extent responsibly acquired, many are to a significant extent non-responsibly acquired, and many are fully non-responsibly acquired.

While fully responsible acquisitions of special connections can increase the lifetime cost you are required to incur in helping others, fully non-responsible acquisitions cannot. It seems implausible that, while someone with no special connections would be required to incur a cost of 10 percent of their time and money to help others, someone whose only special connections are fully non-responsibly acquired would be required to incur a greater cost to help others (at least when adequately helping those to whom they are specially connected doesn't itself require more than 10 percent). For example, if you have a parent with an expensive medical condition, you may be required to help them over strangers as well as required to incur greater costs to help them than you would be required to help strangers. But the fact that you have such a special connection does not plausibly increase how much lifetime cost you are required to incur to help others (assuming you do not need to sacrifice more than 10 percent to adequately help your parent). Like someone with no special connections, you would be required to incur a cost of 10 percent of your time and money to help others. But you would not be required to use as much of this 10 percent on *strangers* as someone with no special connections would be. By contrast, it seems that someone with fully responsibly acquired special connections could be required to incur a cost greater than 10 percent of their time and money to help others, so that at least 10 percent still goes to strangers.

Having distinguished between responsible acquisitions and non-responsible acquisitions, let us next consider what happens if the special connections you have to your friends enhance the permitting reasons to save them without also enhancing the requiring reasons to save them, and then turn to what happens if they enhance requiring reasons. For simplicity, I set aside partially responsible acquisitions and partially non-responsible acquisitions, to see how things work for four "pure" possibilities.

First, suppose that in *Frequent Friend v. Strangers* the special connections you have to your friends enhance the *permitting* reasons to save them without also enhancing the requiring reasons to save them and that these connections are fully *non-responsibly* (but also non-coercively) acquired. And suppose that these special connections enhance the permitting reasons so that it is permissible to save any friend over saving any two strangers. In this case, it is permissible to incur a cost of 10 percent of your time and money to save $N/2$ friends at a cost of $6000 each (assuming there are sufficiently many opportunities to save friends). There is more requiring reason overall to save N strangers than there is to save $N/2$ friends, but there is a sufficiently strong permitting reason to save $N/2$ friends.

Second, suppose that in *Frequent Friend v. Strangers* the special connections you have to your friends enhance the *requiring* reasons to save them and that these connections are fully *non-responsibly* (but also non-coercively) acquired. And suppose that these special connections enhance the requiring reasons so that you are required to save any friend over saving any two strangers. In this case, you are required to incur a cost of at least 10 percent of your time and money to save at least $N/2$ friends at a cost of

$6000 each (assuming there are sufficiently many opportunities to save friends). There is more requiring reason overall to save $N/2$ friends than there is to save N strangers and no sufficiently strong permitting reason to save N strangers.

Third, suppose that in *Frequent Friend v. Strangers* the special connections you have to your friends enhance the *permitting* reasons to save them without also enhancing the requiring reasons to save them and that these connections are fully *responsibly* acquired. And suppose that these special connections enhance the permitting reasons so that it is permissible to save any friend over saving any two strangers. It seems plausible that, given that in *Frequent Stranger v. Strangers* you are required to save at least N strangers at a cost to yourself of at least 10 percent of your time and money, and that in *Frequent Friend v. Strangers* the only special connections you have are fully responsibly acquired, you are in the latter case required to save at least N *people* at a cost of at least 10 percent of your time and money. In sum, you are required to do one of the following: (1) incur a cost of at least 10 percent to save at least N strangers at a cost of $3000 each, (2) incur a cost of at least 20 percent to save at least N friends at a cost of $6000 each, or (3) incur a cost of at least some percentage between 10 and 20 to save a corresponding mixture of friends and strangers, comprising at least N people.[7] Even though there is more requiring reason overall to save $2N$ strangers at a cost of 20 percent than there is to save N friends at this same cost, the special connections to your friends provide a sufficiently strong permitting reason to save them.

Fourth, suppose that in *Frequent Friend v. Strangers* the special connections you have to your friends enhance the *requiring* reasons to save them and that these connections are fully *responsibly* acquired. And suppose that these special connections enhance the requiring reasons so that you're required to save any friend over saving any two strangers. It seems plausible that, given that in *Frequent Stranger v. Strangers* you are required to save at least N strangers at a cost to yourself of at least 10 percent of your time and money, and that in *Frequent Friend v. Strangers* the only special connections you have are fully responsibly acquired, you are in the latter required to save at least N people at a cost to yourself of at least 10 percent of your time and money. But now there is more requiring reason overall to save N friends than there is to save $2N$ strangers and no sufficiently strong permitting reason to save $2N$ strangers. Now you are required to incur a cost of at least 20 percent to save at least N friends (at a cost of $6000 each).

In this section, I have considered how special connections can affect the cost you can be required to incur in helping others over the course of your life. In particular, while responsibly acquired special connections can increase the cost you are required to incur in helping others over the course of your life, non-responsibly acquired special connections cannot. I showed how this works for four "pure" possibilities, corresponding to whether connections are fully responsibly acquired or fully non-responsibly acquired and whether they enhance requiring reasons or permitting reasons. In real-world cases, special connections are partially responsibly acquired and partially non-responsibly acquired, not all special connections are responsibly acquired to the same extent, and some enhance requiring reasons while others enhance permitting reasons. There are more than four possibilities.

Notes

1. On the moral significance of special connections, see Williams 1973, Goodin 1985, Jeske 1998, Brink 2001, Scheffler 2004, Stroud 2010, Kolodny 2010, Keller 2013, and Lange 2020. For skepticism, see Arneson 2003b and Crisp 2018.

2. In addition to the distinction between requiring reasons and permitting reasons, there is a distinction between *cost-requiring* reasons and *conflict-requiring* reasons (see Kamm 1985 and 2021). Suppose you promise A that were it necessary you would sacrifice yourself to save them but do not promise A that you would save them rather than others. This would enhance the cost-requiring reason to save A, but it wouldn't enhance the conflict-requiring reason to save A. If it were between saving A and saving a stranger B to whom you've made no promise, there's no requiring reason to save A rather than B. Alternatively, suppose you promise A that, were it necessary to choose, you would save A rather than B. This would enhance the conflict-requiring reason to save A rather than save B, but it wouldn't enhance the cost-requiring reasons to save A—you could be required to incur just as much cost to save B. As these cases of promising suggest, special connections can enhance one kind of requiring reason without enhancing the other. Perhaps, as the lifeguard on duty at a particular beach, you could be required to incur a much greater cost to save someone from drowning at your beach than you could be required to incur to save 10 people trapped in a burning building one block away from your beach. You may nonetheless be permitted or even required to save the 10 from burning rather than save the one from drowning.

3. For discussion, see Gomberg 1990, Hurka 1997, Fabre 2012, Scheffler 2018, Arneson 2020, and Davis 2021.

4. For more on such issues, see Chapter 2 on full versus partial aggregation, Chapter 5 on diffusion, and relevant citations in each.

5. The amplification effect is plausibly greater when you ignore the *same* friend repeatedly.

6. As with lifetime costs that amplify permitting reasons, there is a range of more specific views we can take here. For example, in the previous chapter I discussed "already done enough" and "will've done enough" interpretations of how incurring costs over a lifetime can amplify permitting reasons not to incur costs on a given occasion. There are analogous views of how forgoing saving friends over a lifetime can amplify requiring reasons to save friends. These can be regarded as views according to which there is an imperfect duty to put your friends first. (This also applies to other special connections beyond friendship.)

7. In variants of this case in which saving friends over strangers would preclude you from saving at least N people, responsibly acquired special connections would not make it permissible to save friends over strangers. It is for this sort of reason that in cases like *Costless Conflict* and *Costly Conflict* (which take place in an imaginary world in which your opportunities to help are very rare) you cannot make it permissible to save the lesser number by responsibly acquiring special connections to them at the time of rescue—say, by promising them that you will save them over the greater number. For relevant discussion, see Bazargan-Forward 2018 and Frowe 2019.

8 | MUST YOU BE AN EFFECTIVE ALTRUIST?

8.1. Back to the Real World

In this final chapter, I draw together the book's main argument: that the "rules of rescue" defended for clean cases in Chapters 1–4 carry over to a significant range of real-world cases in which you can help using time and money. I argue that in the real world there is a *ubiquity of requiring reasons* to help strangers. This may seem overly demanding, but I argue that it isn't, given that there is also a ubiquity of sufficiently strong permitting reasons (section 8.1). I then discuss how to modify the book's main argument, when we drop the assumption that the time, money, and other resources in your possession rightfully belong to you (section 8.2). Next, I define *effective altruism* as the project of using time, money, and other resources to help others the most; and I define an effective altruist as someone who engages in the project of effective altruism to a significant degree (section 8.3). Finally, I turn to whether you are required to be an effective altruist. I argue that a significant proportion of us are required either to be effective altruists or else provide no less help over our lives than

The Rules of Rescue. Theron Pummer, Oxford University Press. © Oxford University Press 2023.
DOI: 10.1093/oso/9780190884147.003.0009

we would have done if we did the minimum required as effective altruists (section 8.4).

In the first four chapters of the book, I defended claims about requiring reasons to help (the greater number) and permitting reasons not to help (the greater number) in a range of clean cases where opportunities to help are very rare. These claims concern how cost and autonomy can make it permissible not to save others; how it can be wrong to save a lesser number of people over a greater number of different people; how it can be wrong to save the lesser number even when it is permissible to save no one; and how, even when it is wrong to save the lesser number, it can be more praiseworthy overall to save the lesser number than to permissibly and blamelessly save no one.

To what extent do these core claims defended in Chapters 1–4 carry over to real-world cases of using time and money to help distant strangers by volunteering, donating to charity, and making a difference with your career? Chapters 5–7 provide a partial answer.

In Chapter 5, I argued that these claims would substantially carry over, if your opportunities to help others were very rare. One potential complication is that, in some *Charity*-like cases, "risky diffusion" may reduce the requiring reason to help. For example, suppose that in *Charity* donating $3000 has a 1/300 chance of saving the lives of 300 strangers. Even though your donation would have the expected value of saving one stranger, it may be that the cost you can be required to incur to bring about a 1/300 chance of saving 300 strangers is significantly less than the cost you can be required to incur to bring about a 99/100 chance of saving one stranger. But just as there remains a strong requiring reason to help in *Risky Diffusion*, there remains a strong requiring reason to donate in such *Charity*-like cases. Moreover, it remains plausible that in these *Charity*-like cases you can be required to save the greater number. For example, there is more requiring reason overall to bring about a 1/300 chance that 600 strangers are saved by donating X to one charity than there is to bring about a 1/300 chance that 300 other strangers are saved by donating X to another charity. This can make it wrong to do the latter even when it is permissible not to donate X at all. Even with the potential complication presented by risky diffusion, core claims from Chapters 1–4 would substantially carry over to real-world cases of using time and money to help distant strangers, *if* your opportunities to help were very rare.

In the real world, your opportunities to help are very frequent—they are constant. At each minute of your life, you can donate to an effective charity or use your time in some similarly helpful way. In Chapter 6, I argued that the high frequency of opportunities to help others can introduce lifetime features that amplify permitting reasons not to help. In Chapter 7, I showed how the permitting reasons and requiring reasons enhanced by special connections can in turn be amplified by lifetime features.

Depending on the degree to which lifetime features can amplify permitting reasons not to help, there is a potentially major disanalogy between cases that occur in an imaginary world in which your opportunities to help are very rare and cases that occur in the real world in which your opportunities to help are very frequent. If there is such a disanalogy, core claims from Chapters 1–4 may not carry over to so many real-world cases of using time and money to help distant strangers.

If a *Pond*-like opportunity to save a stranger's life at little cost to yourself were your only opportunity ever to help anyone, you would be required to save them. But if it were just one of a constant, indefinitely long series of such opportunities, you wouldn't be required to help on every occasion. As argued in Chapter 6, you would instead be required to help on some occasions but not required to help on all occasions. The same holds of *Charity*-like cases. In an imaginary world in which your opportunities to help are very rare, you may be required to give $X in *each* of the very few *Charity*-like cases you come across. But in the real world in which your opportunities to help are very frequent, you may be required to give $X in only a very small percentage of the very many *Charity*-like cases you come across.

This effect of living in a world in which your opportunities to help are very frequent is likewise reflected in requirements to save the greater number. For instance, when you face an indefinitely long series of opportunities either to save the lesser number or at slightly greater cost save the greater number, it can turn out that you are required to save the greater number on some occasions but not required to do so on all occasions.

The proportion of occasions on which you are required to help (the greater number) depends on the number of opportunities to help at cost you would have over the course of your life as well as on the degree to which lifetime features can amplify permitting reasons not to help (the greater number). These lifetime considerations therefore partially determine the extent to which core claims from Chapters 1–4 carry over to cases that occur in the real world, where your opportunities to help are very frequent.

Chapters 5–7 show how several factors fail to prevent core claims defended in earlier chapters from carrying over to real-world cases of using time and money to help distant strangers by volunteering, donating to charity, and making a difference with your career. At the same time, they show how factors like risky diffusion and frequency can complicate the ways in which these core claims carry over.

Property rights present a further potential complication. Are there (cost-based or autonomy-based) permitting reasons not to "donate" things in your possession that are not rightfully yours? Most of the cases in Chapters 1–4 involve sacrificing your limbs to save others, and it seems clear that your body is rightfully yours. It is less clear to what extent the time, money, and other resources in your (physical or legal) possession rightfully belong to you. So far, I have avoided this complication by operating on the assumption that these things are rightfully yours. But even if most of the time, money, and other resources in your possession do not rightfully belong to you, presumably a significant portion still does. So, while property rights may further complicate the ways in which core claims from Chapters 1–4 carry over to real-world cases of helping strangers using time and money, these claims could for all that carry over to a significant extent. Section 8.2 of this chapter discusses how to modify the book's main argument, when we drop the assumption that the time, money, and other resources in your possession rightfully belong to you.

In Chapter 5, I argued that the fact that real-world cases like *Charity* involve uncertainty about whether your act will help or harm does not by itself prevent core claims from Chapters 1–4 from carrying over to real-world cases of using time and money to help distant strangers. Nonetheless, what proportion of real-world cases these core claims carry over to depends on the degree of uncertainty that your act will help or harm.

Undoubtedly there are plenty of real-world cases like *Charity* in which the chance of helping is low enough and the chance of doing harm is high enough that there is requiring reason overall *not* to donate to the charity in question. This is especially likely to happen if, as seems plausible, there is stronger requiring reason not to do harm than there is to help (prevent harm). So even when a charity "helps more than it harms" it can still be that there is requiring reason overall not to donate to it. As a crude illustration, there is more requiring reason overall not to donate than there is to donate when donating would bring about a 50 percent chance of saving 101 lives with a 50 percent chance of killing 100 others as a side effect. Given that there is a moral constraint against doing harm, it can be wrong to donate even when standard act conse-quentialism implies that donating is required.

There is empirical evidence that some charities effectively help distant strangers and with a fairly low risk of doing harm. Among them are charities that prevent or treat tropical diseases like malaria, schistosomiasis, and trachoma. There is good reason to believe that some of these charities help much more per dol-lar donated than others. However, charities that directly prevent or treat diseases also risk creating incentives for governments to deprioritize these diseases, indirectly doing harm in the long run.[1] My sense is that some such charities are sufficiently low-risk and sufficiently helpful in expectation that it remains permissible to give to them. Nonetheless, even when it is permissible to give to a charity that carries a risk of doing harm, it may be permissible to instead give to a less risky charity even if it is much less helpful in expectation. (Perhaps it is permissible to bring about a 75 percent chance of saving 100 lives with a 5 percent chance of killing 10 others as a side effect but also permissible to instead bring about a 50 percent chance of saving 50 lives with no chance of killing anyone.)

It may well be that there is requiring reason overall not to donate to most charities that have the aim of helping distant strangers living in extreme poverty. But not all such charities are so bad. Some are very good, and plausibly no worse than any other charity.

Even if I were mistaken about this—and there were *no* charities with the aim of helping distant strangers in extreme poverty that are sufficiently low-risk and sufficiently helpful in expectation—there would remain many *other* opportunities to help. For example, you could donate to or volunteer for charities that work on reforming the criminal justice system. You could donate to or volunteer for charities that reduce animal suffering on factory farms. You could donate to or volunteer for charities that focus on existential risks posed by climate change, pandemics, nuclear weapons, or artificial intelligence. Or you could donate to or volunteer for charities that research the effectiveness of charities. Even if there were no permissible ways to help strangers in extreme poverty, there would remain other ways you could use money or time to effectively help strangers, with a low enough risk of doing harm.[2]

In the real world, there is a ubiquity of opportunities to use time or money to help strangers. There is a ubiquity of cases in which the requiring reasons to help by preventing significant harm more than amply outweigh the requiring reasons not to help (if there are any). These opportunities differ substantially in terms of how much they help per dollar or hour spent. And these opportunities are present constantly throughout your life. At least whenever what there is most requiring reason overall to do is not already determined by other considerations like moral constraints or special connections, it *will* be determined by the ubiquity of opportunities to help.

With a ubiquity of opportunities to help comes a *ubiquity of requiring reasons*. As argued in Chapter 6, given that there is a strong requiring reason to help in *NearPlus*, there is an equally strong requiring reason to help at each minute in *Frequent NearPlus*. Similarly, if in an imaginary world in which your opportunities to help are very rare there is a strong requiring reason to donate $3000 to a malaria charity to bring about a 1/300 chance that 300 strangers will be saved, then in a more realistic world in which there is a ubiquity of such opportunities to help there is an equally strong requiring reason to donate $3000 on each occasion (in real-world cases, the ubiquity of requiring reasons to help by donating will often be accompanied by other sorts of requiring reasons, such as those stemming from moral constraints and special connections).

The ubiquity of requiring reasons to help may seem overly demanding. There is constantly most requiring reason overall to be helping. It is wrong not to help on any given occasion unless there is a sufficiently strong permitting reason not to help on that occasion. It's as if you're constantly under threat of a vast tide of requiring reasons overtaking the breakwater of permitting reasons protecting you.[3]

While this may initially appear overly demanding, I believe the arguments and resources presented throughout this book show such an appearance to be mistaken. We need to take account of the full range of permitting reasons. The ubiquity of requiring reasons might have been overly demanding, if the only permitting reasons were cost-based; but there are also those based on autonomy and special connections. The ubiquity of requiring reasons might still have been overly demanding, if the permitting reasons not to help on a particular occasion were based solely on the sacrifice made in helping on this particular occasion. Then, while there would be a ubiquity of permitting reasons not to help, they would only rarely be sufficiently strong. But, as argued in Chapter 6, there are lifetime features that amplify various sorts of permitting reasons. As long as you will have done enough, there is a ubiquity of *sufficiently strong* permitting reasons. In a substantial portion of the very many occasions on which it is possible for you to help, lifetime features can make it permissible not to help when it would otherwise be wrong not to. They can make it permissible for you to "switch off" from helping strangers, instead turning your attention to your own personal projects and plans. The breakwater of permitting reasons can be built up enough to withstand the vast tide of requiring reasons to help.

Still, the breakwater cannot plausibly be built up so far that you're never required to help. Requiring reasons and permitting reasons interact so that, in a significant range of real-world cases, it is wrong not to use time and money to help, as well as wrong to help a lesser number of strangers rather than comparably help a greater number of other strangers. Indeed, they interact so that, in a significant range of real-world cases, it is wrong to use an amount of time or money in a way that helps less rather than helps much more, even when it is permissible not to use this time or money to help. It can be wrong to donate $X (or Y hours) to one charity instead of donating $X (or Y hours) to another charity that saves on average twice as many lives per dollar (or hour) donated, even when it is permissible not to donate $X (or Y hours). This is more likely to happen when your connection to the less cost-effective charity is no stronger than your connection to the more cost-effective charity. As cases like *Cancer v. Malaria* suggest, sometimes special connections make it permissible to donate time or money to less cost-effective charities rather than more cost-effective ones. But special connections don't always carry the day. It can be wrong to donate $X to a cancer charity to which you have only a very weak special connection, instead of donating $X to a malaria charity to which you have no special connection, when the latter saves on average twice as many lives per dollar donated. For example, being "challenged" by an acquaintance over social media to contribute to a particular cause is unlikely to be a sufficiently strong special connection, though it may make this cause salient.

Many will at least initially find it counterintuitive that the rules of clean rescue cases *ever* apply to real-world cases of volunteering or donating; even if it's wrong to save one drowning stranger rather than save two others, it may seem that it can't be wrong to donate a large sum of money to charity just because you could have donated it to a different charity that's twice as cost-effective. I believe the cases and arguments presented throughout this book reveal this to be an illusion. The core claims about clean rescue cases defended in Chapters 1–4 do carry over to a significant range of real-world cases in which you can help using time and money. The messiness of the real world creates imprecision or at least uncertainty about the extent of this range.

8.2. Property Rights

Throughout this book I make the simplifying assumption that the time, money, and other resources in your possession rightfully belong to you. In this section, I discuss how to modify the book's main argument when we drop this assumption.

Suppose some resource X is rightfully yours, in that you have a moral right to X. Then the fact that sacrificing X in the course of helping strangers is costly to you is a cost-based permitting reason not to help. And the fact that sacrificing X in the course of helping makes a difference to how your life unfolds is an autonomy-based permitting reason not to help. It is much less plausible that these facts are permitting reasons when X is not rightfully yours.

Dropping the assumption that the time, money, and other resources in your possession rightfully belong to you will not substantially affect the main arguments developed *within* Chapters 1–4. These arguments need only appeal to cases involving sacrificing limbs to save others, and it seems clear enough that such personal resources as your body parts rightfully belong to you. And, at least in the absence of agreements or contracts to the contrary, "your time" similarly rightfully belongs to you in the sense that you have a moral right to use your mind and body over time as you choose. These claims aren't being *assumed* in order to avoid complications. They are intuitive enough to assert as provisionally correct.

It is less clear to what extent the money and other external resources in your possession (your aspirin, clothes, and car) rightfully belong to you. Whether these resources rightfully belong to you depends on which view of distributive justice is correct, a question beyond the scope of this book.[4] As a brief illustration of this dependence and its significance for the book's main argument, consider two views of distributive justice.

First consider an *egalitarian* view according to which each person has a moral right to a fair share of the world's resources, so that each person enjoys equal opportunities for well-being. On this view, whatever constitutes your fair share of money and other external resources is rightfully yours, as are particular objects that you freely purchase using your fair share of resources.

Next consider a *libertarian* view according to which you have a moral right to a share of the world's resources either acquired by you from nature without thereby making others worse off, or freely transferred to you by others who acquired resources in this way. This share of resources is rightfully yours, as are particular objects that you freely purchase using it.

These are certainly not the only views of distributive justice; some views are neither egalitarian nor libertarian, and some views are pluralist in that they incorporate egalitarian, libertarian, and other elements. The egalitarian view and the libertarian view nonetheless illustrate a disagreement about what portion of money and other external resources in your possession is rightfully yours. The libertarian view could imply that, while resources worth $10 billion are rightfully yours from birth, resources worth only $100 are rightfully mine from birth (perhaps your ancestors acquired resources without making others worse off, whereas my ancestors acquired resources in ways that made others worse off). By contrast, the egalitarian view could imply that each person's fair share of the world's resources is worth $1 million.

With either view of distributive justice in place, we can approximate what portion of the money and other external resources in your possession is rightfully yours. When using the portion of these resources that is rightfully yours in the course of helping others is costly to you, there is a cost-based permitting reason not to help. But when using the portion of these resources that is not rightfully yours in the course of helping others, the fact that doing so would be costly to you is not plausibly a cost-based permitting reason not to help. If cost still provided a cost-based permitting reason not to help, it would presumably be substantially diminished. Similar remarks apply to autonomy-based permitting reasons.

The book's main argument is that the core claims from Chapters 1–4, about requiring reasons to help the most and permitting reasons not to, carry over to a significant range of real-world cases in which you can help using time and money. The real world presents a ubiquity of opportunities to help, bringing with it a ubiquity of requiring reasons. You're constantly under threat of a vast tide of requiring reasons overtaking the breakwater of permitting reasons protecting you. I argued that the breakwater of permitting reasons can be built up enough to withstand the vast tide of requiring reasons to help. Dropping the simplifying assumption that the time, money, and other resources in your possession rightfully belong to you, then, will *lower the breakwater*. In the real world, in which a substantial portion of the money and other external resources in your possession may not be rightfully yours, the "ubiquity of sufficiently strong permitting reasons" may not be quite so ubiquitous after all. You would then be required to help the most in a wider range of cases than you would if all the resources in your possession were rightfully yours. Dropping the simplifying assumption may also *raise the tide*. Resources that are not rightfully yours may instead rightfully belong to others so that there are requiring reasons of justice to transfer them to the rightful individuals or groups. Reasons of distributive justice and rectificatory justice may not always coincide with doing whatever helps the most, though I suspect there will be substantial overlap when it comes to helping people in extreme poverty. What to do when reasons of justice conflict with reasons to help the most is beyond the scope of this book. While reasons of justice are often weightier, it seems that reasons to help are weightier in a significant range of cases.

Is there no limit to how far the breakwater could be lowered? What if the world's resources were so scarce that a fair share of them were worth only a penny? What if your ancestors stole land from indigenous peoples or used slave labor to harvest the land? Then egalitarian views and libertarian views alike may imply that virtually none of the money or other external resources in your possession is rightfully yours. Even if there remained strong permitting reasons not to use your body or time to help strangers at cost to yourself, there may be virtually no permitting reasons not to use the money or other external resources in your possession to help strangers at cost to yourself.

I find it plausible that you are permitted to hang onto a share of resources, including money, when necessary for living a life that is minimally decent in terms of well-being and autonomy.[5] It seems permissible to hang onto such a *minimum share* of resources even when this share is much more substantial than what's rightfully yours according to egalitarian and libertarian views of the sorts mentioned above. One way to defend this claim is to hold that the resources in your possession that are necessary for living a minimally decent life are in virtue of this rightfully yours—including when there aren't enough resources in the world for everyone to have a minimum share.[6] Another way to defend this claim is to hold that, even when the minimum share of resources in your possession is not rightfully yours, there is still a sufficiently strong permitting reason not to sacrifice it for others. In general, when X is not rightfully yours, the fact that sacrificing X in the course of helping strangers is costly to you is not a permitting reason not to help. But an exception is made when X is necessary for you to live a minimally decent life.

8.3. Effective Altruism

Effective altruism is the project of using time, money, and other resources to help others the most.[7] In that this is a book about the moral reasons and requirements to use time, money, and other resources in ways that help others the most, it is a book about the moral reasons and requirements to engage in effective altruism.

Helping "others" is meant to include at least all innocent persons, regardless of their gender, race, nationality, and so forth, and regardless of any special connections to you. We may expand "others" to include possible future persons, as well as animals that are sentient but lack other mental capacities of persons. Although in this book I focus on reasons to help persons, many of my claims also apply to helping sentient animals that are not persons.

Helping others "the most" involves *helping a greater number* of people over a lesser number of people (in conflict cases as well as in no-conflict cases) when the amount of help you can provide for each is the same. And it involves *providing more help for each* over less help for each (in conflict cases as well as in no-conflict cases) when the number you can help is the same. But it plausibly involves more than this. It plausibly involves trading off dimensions of helping—so that, for example, you help "the most" by helping a much larger number of people to a somewhat lesser extent each over helping a much smaller number of people to a somewhat greater extent each. Effective altruism is not uniquely tied to helping others the most in a "fully aggregative" sense (see Chapter 2). It seems that helping the most in either a fully aggregative sense or a partially aggregative sense would qualify as engaging in the project of effective altruism.

Questions of aggregation and cost-effectiveness are familiar in global health.[8] Using limited funds, should we prevent a few malaria deaths, cure a greater number of nonlethal parasitic infections, or provide a still greater number of sight-restoring surgeries? Life-saving interventions are not always what help the most "in aggregate." Preventing many serious nonlethal harms may help more than saving a life. And when "saving a life" involves merely prolonging it for a very short while, it may be more helpful to prevent just one serious nonlethal harm instead.

Given the wide variety of ways you can help others, it may be that in nearly all cases there is no single alternative that helps others the most. You can donate to charities that provide medical care to those in extreme poverty or to charities that work on reforming the criminal justice system or to charities that reduce animal suffering on factory farms or to charities that focus on existential risks, and so on. The differences between what these charities do can make it difficult or impossible to determine which there is most requiring reason overall to support. One possibility is that, within the "cause area" of global health, there is a charity that helps the most and that, within the cause area of animal suffering, there is a charity that helps the most, and so on—but no charity that helps the most across all cause areas. To be clear, we can make many reasonable comparisons across cause areas, and indeed some cause areas are better than others. But among the best cause areas, we may end up with an "upper set" of charities, each of which helps the most within its cause area and none of which helps more than (or precisely as much as) any other charity in this set. Even when there is nothing that helps the most, there may still be something that helps *no less* than anything else.[9]

The project of effective altruism can be engaged in to greater or lesser degrees. Resources like time and money can be used to help others to a greater or lesser extent, depending on the quantity of resources directed toward helping others ("altruism") and depending on the extent to which this portion of resources is directed in ways that help more rather than less ("effectiveness"). For example, you can help more by giving more to charity and by allocating what you do give to more cost-effective charities.

An *effective altruist*, then, is someone who engages in the project of effective altruism to a *significant* degree. Most, if not all, real-life effective altruists have many projects besides effective altruism—few, if any, have effective altruism as their sole project. To be an effective altruist, you need only to engage in the project of effective altruism to a significant degree. You need not engage in it maximally.[10] And it is vague what a "significant" degree amounts to. On one plausible way of making "significant" more precise, you need to allocate at least 1 percent of your time and money to helping others the most, to qualify as an effective altruist; on another, you need to allocate at least 10 percent (assuming you are roughly as well off as a typical member of an affluent country). Some ways of making "significant" precise are implausible—clearly, you need not allocate 100 percent of your time and money to helping others the most to qualify as an effective altruist. Similarly, it is doubtful you can allocate much less than 1 percent and still qualify.[11] Finally, since you needn't join the effective altruist community to significantly engage in the project of using time and money to help others the most, you can be an effective altruist without participating in the community.

8.4. Must You Be an Effective Altruist?

Are you required to be an effective altruist? One possibility is that, just as there is a ubiquity of requiring reasons to help others, so too is there a ubiquity of comparably strong requiring reasons to fight social injustice. Then, rather than allocating a significant portion of time and money to *helping others* the most, it could be permissible to allocate a significant portion of time and money to fighting social injustice the most. In this way, you may not be required to be an effective altruist. We could still ask whether you are required to allocate a significant portion of time and money *either* to helping others the most *or* to fighting social injustice the most.[12] To simplify, I'll here count fighting social injustice as a form of helping others (preventing significant harm to others).

Are you required to allocate a significant portion of time and money to helping others the most? Must you be an effective altruist? There are several factors relevant here. They include the amount of help you can provide per dollar or hour donated, the cost to you per dollar or hour donated (and the difference made to how your life unfolds per dollar or hour donated), the lifetime well-being you would be left with as a result of helping, the kinds and degrees of connections to those you can help, the relative strength of the requiring reasons to help and the permitting reasons not to, and whether a multiplier view or an absolute limit view is correct. Moreover, I often write "time and money" as if they were interchangeable, but cost-based permitting reasons and autonomy-based permitting reasons may function quite differently depending on whether you help using time (volunteering or making a difference with your career) or money (donating to charity). As noted in section 8.2, it may be that while your time is rightfully yours, much of the money in your possession isn't. And choosing where to volunteer or what career to go into may make a much bigger difference to how your life unfolds than choosing where to donate, triggering correspondingly stronger autonomy-based permitting reasons. Even if you would save many more lives as a philanthropist banker than as a humanitarian doctor, and even if in addition it would be better *for you* to be a banker, you could still have a sufficiently strong autonomy-based permitting reason to be a doctor.

Even if we had all the empirical details of your life, we may be unable to say with confidence how much time and money you are required to spend helping others. And there may be no precise answer. In addition, the relevant empirical details of your life may differ from mine. If I am much wealthier than you, then donating will typically cost you more well-being than it will cost me, dollar for dollar.[13] If you have a parent with an expensive medical condition and I don't, then you may not be required to sacrifice as much to help strangers as I would be (as noted in the previous chapter, it seems implausible that you would have to sacrifice as much to help strangers as I would, in addition to what you have to sacrifice to help those to whom you have non-responsibly acquired special connections).

For a significant proportion of us—at least those of us who are roughly as well off as a typical member of an affluent country and who do not have unusually demanding non-responsibly acquired special connections—it seems that requiring us to spend only 1 percent of our time and money on helping others is too permissive and that requiring 50 percent is too demanding. To keep things simple, let's go with tithing. Let us suppose, as seems plausible, that a significant proportion of us are required to spend at least 10 percent of our time and money helping others and that, if we do the minimum required by allocating exactly 10 percent, we must allocate it in the most cost-effective way available—that is, in a way that provides no less help than any other way available.

For many of us, the relevant baseline lifetime requirement will be lower or higher than 10 percent. The analysis offered below can be transposed accordingly.

Given all this, it may seem that a significant proportion of us are required to be effective altruists, as defined above. After all, allocating 10 percent of your time and money to helping others the most would seem to qualify as engaging in effective altruism to a significant degree.

However, even if you are required to use at least 10 percent of your resources to help others and to help most cost-effectively if you give exactly 10 percent, it is not clear that you are required to be an effective altruist. Effectiveness is a central component of effective altruism. To engage in the project of effective altruism to a significant degree, you need to both direct a significant percentage of resources toward helping others *and* use this portion of resources to help others significantly cost-effectively. Someone who uses only a minuscule percentage of resources helping very cost-effectively is not an effective *altruist*. At the same time, someone who uses a massive percentage of resources helping very cost-*in*effectively is not an *effective* altruist.

If you do the minimum required by allocating exactly 10 percent to helping others, you must allocate it in the most cost-effective way available. Is it permissible to help others less cost-effectively, as long as you allocate a greater percentage accordingly? For example, can you help *half* as cost-effectively if you allocate 20 percent, thereby providing no less help (suppose you would save N lives either way)? It may seem that you can. Other things being equal, it is permissible to incur a greater rather than lesser cost to yourself and to choose either of two alternatives when

202 The Rules of Rescue

neither provides more help than the other. So, why shouldn't you be allowed to incur greater costs in helping less cost-effectively, as long as this provides no less help?

Suppose that, rather than saving N people by allocating 10 percent at maximal cost-effectiveness, you save N others by allocating 20 percent at half cost-effectiveness. Whether this is permissible depends on whether there is a sufficiently strong permitting reason to help half as cost-effectively, using 20 percent, instead of using the same amount to help most cost-effectively. If the cost is the same either way, there is no cost-based permitting reason to use 20 percent half as cost-effectively. And when the only significant difference between these two ways of using 20 percent is whether N people are helped or at least $2N$ others are helped, there is no significant autonomy-based permitting reason to use it less cost-effectively. In this case, it would be wrong to allocate 20 percent at half cost-effectiveness, even though this would provide no less help than doing the minimum required by allocating 10 percent at maximal cost-effectiveness. (Similarly, in *Costly Conflict*, it is wrong to save the lesser number at great cost to yourself, even though this would provide no less help than doing the minimum required by saving no one.)

Again, it seems there are important differences between time and money. Absent special connections, donating money to one charity rather than another does not itself make a significant difference to how your life unfolds. In such cases, there is no significant autonomy-based permitting reason to use $X to help N people when you could have instead used it to help at least $2N$ others. But, since spending years of your life working in one career rather than another may constitute a significant difference in how your life unfolds, there may be a significant autonomy-based permitting reason to use X years to help N people when you could have instead used it to help at least $2N$ others. In this way, it can turn out that, rather than using 10 percent of your time to help others in the most cost-effective way available, it is permissible to instead use 20 percent of your time to help half as cost-effectively, as long as this provides no less help. Autonomy-based permitting reasons to use our time as we choose therefore generate a significant range of real-world cases in which we can do the minimum required either by being effective altruists or by helping much less cost-effectively but at a much greater cost to ourselves, so as to provide no less help over the course of our lives than if we did the minimum required as effective altruists.

Special connections expand the range of cases like this and apply to the use of money as well as time. If you have strong enough special connections to particular people, causes, or charities, it can turn out that, rather than using 10 percent of your money and time to help others in the most cost-effective way available (helping N people), it is permissible to instead use 20 percent of your money and time to help half as cost-effectively, as long as this provides no less help (e.g., helping N others each to the same extent). Depending on whether they give rise to requiring reasons or permitting reasons, these special connections could either make it the case that there is more requiring reason overall to use 20 percent of your time and money to help N people to whom you are specially connected rather than help $2N$ others or else make it the case that there is a sufficiently strong permitting reason to do so. Similarly, it could be permissible to use 30 percent to help N

people rather than help $3N$ others, were the relevant special connections proportionately stronger.

It is important to again distinguish between responsibly acquired special connections and non-responsibly acquired special connections. As noted in the previous chapter, it seems implausible that, while someone with no special connections would be required to incur a cost of 10 percent of their time and money to help others, someone whose only special connections are fully non-responsibly acquired would be required to incur a greater cost to help others (at least when adequately helping those to whom they are specially connected doesn't itself require more than 10 percent). But it seems that someone with fully responsibly acquired special connections could be required to incur a cost greater than 10 percent, so that at least 10 percent still goes to strangers.

If you have sufficiently demanding non-responsibly acquired special connections, you may end up required to spend nearly all your time and money helping a relatively small group of people. Then doing the minimum required would involve not only not being an effective altruist but also providing less help than you would have done if you had been an effective altruist (though requirements of effectiveness would still apply when helping those to whom you have special connections).

Partly for this reason, I claim only that a *significant proportion* of us are required either to be effective altruists or else to provide no less help than we would have done if we did the minimum required as effective altruists. A significant proportion of us are required to spend at least 10 percent of our time and money helping others, and if we do the minimum required by allocating exactly 10 percent to helping others, we must allocate it in the most cost-effective way available. Special connections and autonomy-based permitting reasons can make it permissible for us to instead help much less than maximally cost-effectively but at a much greater cost to ourselves so as to provide no less help over the course of our lives than if we did the minimum required as effective altruists (e.g., we could give 15 percent, half at maximal cost-effectiveness and half at half cost-effectiveness, or give 40 percent, all at one-quarter cost-effectiveness, and so on).

Whether those of us who are required to spend at least 10 percent of our time and money helping others are required to be effective altruists depends on the availability of adequate special connections and autonomy-based permitting reasons. Since these are typically available in the real world, we are not typically required to be effective altruists. Still, we are required to provide no less help than we would have done if we did the minimum required as effective altruists. We are permitted to do this by being effective altruists, but few of us are required to do this by being effective altruists.

Even if you are not required to be an effective altruist, I hope this book makes it clear enough that your altruism is nonetheless significantly constrained by requirements of effectiveness, including when altruism is not required. For example, when the connection you have to a less cost-effective charity is no stronger than the connection you have to a more cost-effective charity, it can be wrong to give a sum of money to the less cost-effective charity rather than the more cost-effective charity, even when you are permitted not to give this sum to charity at all. When the connection you have to a less cost-effective charity is stronger than the connection you have to a more cost-effective charity, there can be a permitting reason of some strength to give to the less cost-effective charity. Whether a permitting reason is sufficiently strong on a given occasion will depend on a variety of factors, including life-time features. If over the course of your life you face a very large number of choices of whether to help more or less and there is on each occasion a permitting reason of some strength to help less, lifetime features can make it the case that you are sometimes permitted to help less.

In practice, "ineffective altruism" is often attributable to ignorance of the relevant differences in cost-effectiveness. When that ignorance is permissible or excusable, ineffective altruism is not blameworthy and may be praiseworthy. But often ineffective altruism is instead or in addition attributable to somewhat blameworthy forms of indifference to effectiveness (e.g., "innumerate altruism" or "imbalanced altruism").[14] Even when it is, the arguments in Chapter 4 imply that it can nonetheless be praiseworthy overall. These arguments have the further implication that, even when an instance of ineffective altruism is wrong and to some extent blameworthy, it can nonetheless be *more* praiseworthy overall than a non-altruistic alternative that is permissible and blameless.

When you find yourself engaged in ineffective altruism that is not permissible, you should not focus entirely on your conduct's negative aspect and not only because of the counterproductivity of doing so. Your conduct may not only be praiseworthy overall but considerably more so than the permissible non-altruism of many others. At the same time, you should not lose sight of the fact that your conduct is wrong and has a blameworthy aspect. The ideal response to such ineffective altruism is mixed, a proportionate reflection of both the praiseworthy as well as blameworthy aspects of your conduct. When such an ideal response is impossible or psychologically infeasible, you may have to navigate between under-blaming yourself and under-praising yourself.

When it comes to your responses to the wrong yet overall praiseworthy ineffective altruism of others, these matters are arguably more delicate still. For instance, even when someone is blameworthy overall for performing some act, we can lack the *standing* to blame them for it.[15] If you are an ineffective altruist, it may seem hypocritical or inappropriate of you to blame me for engaging in *ineffective* altruism, even if at the same time you greatly praise me for my altruism. But suppose that you are an effective altruist using 10 percent of your time and money helping maximally cost-effectively and I am an ineffective altruist using 60 percent of my time and money helping half as cost-effectively, thereby providing three times as much help as you. Suppose, however, that I do *not* have a sufficiently strong permitting reason to do this rather than use my 60 percent maximally cost-effectively, so that I provide six times as much help as you. In this case, I do not believe it would be inappropriate of you to blame me (as part of a mixed response involving considerable praise) for engaging in ineffective altruism, even though, thanks my great sacrifice, I help others to a much greater extent than you. Of course, even if you have the standing to blame me, it is a further question whether you should, all things considered.

Notes

1. See Wenar 2011, Deaton 2013 (chapter 7), Pummer 2016b, Temkin 2019, MacAskill 2019b, and Côté and Steuwer 2022.

2. If you're considering using time to help, I'd recommend https://80000ho urs.org/. And if you're considering using money to help, I'd recommend https://www.givewell.org/ or https://funds.effectivealtruism.org/. On helping animals, see DeGrazia 1996, Višak and Garner 2015, Korsgaard 2018, and Kagan 2019. On the longterm future and reducing existential risks, see Ord 2020, Pummer 2020, and MacAskill forthcoming. On the moral value of information, see Askell 2019. On challenges of "cluelessness" posed by the inscrutability of the long-term indirect effects of our acts, see Lenman 2000, Greaves 2016, and Mogensen 2021. For political critiques of contemporary philanthropy, see Lechterman 2021 and Saunders-Hastings 2022.

3. The breakwater metaphor is from Sinclair 2018 (45).

4. The literature on this topic is vast. See, for example, Rawls 1971, Nozick 1974, Temkin 1993, Parfit 1997, Anderson 1999, Arneson 2000, Murphy and Nagel 2002, Otsuka 2003, Fried 2004, Casal 2007, Quong 2011, and Woollard 2015 (chapter 8). For an overview, see Lamont and Favor 2017.

5. I here draw upon Shue 1980 and Fabre 2012 (18–23).

6. For a related view, see Quong 2020 (91–92).

7. For an introduction to effective altruism, see https://www.effectivealtru ism.org/ and MacAskill 2015. My focus here is the *project* of effective altruism, rather than the *social movement* (for discussion of the latter, see Berg 2018, Berkey 2020 and 2021). The project-based definition offered here is a revised version of the one found in MacAskill and Pummer 2020 (2), according to which effective altruism is "the *project* of using evidence and reason to try to find out how to do the most good, and on this basis trying to do the most good" (based on MacAskill 2019a [15–17]). The definition proposed in the main text here replaces "doing good" with "helping others." This is largely to retain promoting the well-being of individuals as the project's aim—promoting "the good" may encompass too much for the project to remain sufficiently unified. For simplicity, my proposed definition also omits the "finding out how to do the most good" element. Finding out how to help others the most seems to be part of the project of effective altruism only if it is part of helping others the most. At

the same time, it seems we need a suitably evidence-relative interpretation of "helping others the most," for it seems you are engaged in effective altruism if *relative to your evidence* you help others the most, even if *in fact* you fail to help others at all.

8. See, for example, Kamm 2013 (part IV) and Ord 2019.

9. The idea of an "upper set" of charities is noted in Pummer 2016a (85). It may be that the charities in this set are "on a par" or "incommensurable" with each other (see Chang 2002 and Rabinowicz 2012). More radically, it may be that "helps more than" is an intransitive relation, allowing for the possibility that *A* helps more than *B*, *B* helps more than *C*, and *C* helps more than *A* (see Temkin 2012). In such a scenario, not only is there no alternative that helps *the most*, but there is no alternative that helps *no less than any other*. There can still be an upper set even in this scenario (see Schwartz 1972 and Ross 2015).

10. You are required *not* to be a "maximal" effective altruist, if that involves *always* helping others the most. After all, you can be required not to help others the most when this conflicts with moral constraints against harming, stealing, lying, and so forth. Of course, effective altruists do not standardly recommend being maximal effective altruists of such a morally unconstrained sort.

11. What counts as a plausible way of making "significant" precise is partly determined by how the term "effective altruist" is used in practice, particularly by those in the effective altruism community. There may also be pragmatic reasons to "engineer" the concept of an effective altruist to be more or less inclusive in terms of how much you have to engage in the project of effective altruism to qualify (see MacAskill 2019a).

12. On requiring reasons to fight social injustice, see Crisp and Pummer 2020. As with opportunities to help others, opportunities to fight social injustice differ substantially in terms of how much they decrease social injustice per dollar or hour spent. And there is more requiring reason to do what decreases social injustice to a greater extent, other things being equal.

13. For an empirically informed discussion of how well-being relates to money and the implications for what the affluent are required to give, see MacAskill et al. 2018. And on what kinds of cost can permit not helping, see Barry and Lawford-Smith 2019.

14. For explanations of ineffective altruism, see Bloom 2016, Burum et al. 2020, Caviola et al. 2020 and 2021, and Caviola and Schubert unpublished.

15. See, for instance, Wallace 2010, Bell 2013, Todd 2019, and Bowen unpublished. Also see Nelkin 2022 on asymmetries between self-blame and other-blame.

GLOSSARY OF CASES

- *Accident*: While out for a hike in a country you have never been to before, you see on the map of your phone a red dot indicating that there is an emergency about 1000 miles away from you. You tap the dot for a brief description of the situation. It turns out that a boulder is hurtling toward stranger *B*. The remaining details are just like those in *Injustice*, except that *B*'s plight is the result of a mere accident (rather than social injustice)—*B* has to take the same risky route to work as *A*, but on this occasion *B* isn't on the risky route.

- *Accident v. Injustice*: You can save one stranger or two others. The one stranger's plight is the result of a mere accident, whereas the plights of two others are the result of social injustice.

- *Alone*: While out for a hike in a country you have never been to before, you see on the map of your phone a red dot indicating that there is an emergency about 1000 miles away from you. You tap the dot for a brief description of the situation. It turns out that a boulder is hurtling toward stranger *A*, who is stuck in the boulder's path. You realize that you can save *A*'s life using your phone. For $X you can tap a button on the screen of your phone that causes a large bulldozer to move in front of the boulder, saving *A* without doing any damage to the bulldozer. *No one else can help* A.

- *Alone v. Many*: You are the only person who can save one stranger, whereas you are one among many others who can save two other strangers (and you are certain no one else will save these two other strangers).

- *Bored v. Joyful*: Two strangers, Bored and Joyful, face a deadly threat. You can do nothing, save Bored's life at no cost to yourself, or save Joyful's life at no cost to yourself. You cannot save both. So far each has lived a boring, somewhat empty life. If Bored is saved, their life will go on in this fashion. But, if Joyful is saved, their life will change for much the better. If saved, each would live another 40 years. While Bored's remaining life would be decent, Joyful's would contain much more of what makes life worth living.

- *Cancer v. Malaria*: Over the course of your whole life, you will have only one opportunity to help others. When this opportunity arises, you can help in only one of two ways. You can either donate $X to a cancer charity that on average saves one life per $X donated or instead donate $X to a malaria charity that on average saves two lives per $X donated. When you lost a parent to cancer a few years ago, you acquired the central life project of helping cancer victims. You have really wanted to advance this project, but you have not yet had a chance to do so. Now is your only chance. Also, you recently accidentally ingested an antidepressant that makes the psychological costs of not donating to the cancer charity roughly equivalent to the psychological costs of not donating to the malaria charity.

- *Charity*: There are malaria charities operating in areas of extreme poverty that save on average one life for every $3000 they receive. You can donate to such a charity right now by visiting a website and entering your credit card details.

- *Closed Diffusion*: While out for a hike in a country you have never been to before, you see on the map of your phone a red dot indicating that there is an emergency about 1000 miles away from you. You tap the dot for a brief description of the situation. There are 300 boulders about to crush 300 strangers, one boulder per stranger. There are 300 bulldozers that can stop the boulders, one bulldozer per boulder. If activated, a bulldozer will move into the path of its corresponding boulder, bringing about a 99 percent chance of stopping it. For $X you can tap a button on the screen of your phone that will certainly activate *one or another* of the bulldozers, and there is an equal (1/300) chance of any bulldozer in particular being the one to get activated. *Each particular stranger would get a 1/300 (times 99/100) chance of being saved, and there is a 99 percent chance that some stranger or other would be saved.* Many other people can similarly help these strangers, but you are certain none of them will.

- *Concentration*: As in *Closed Diffusion*, except now you are only able to help *one of the strangers in particular*. For $X you can bring about a 99 percent chance that this particular stranger is saved.

- *Concentration v. Closed Diffusion*: You can either pay $X to give one particular stranger a 99 percent chance of being saved or instead pay $X to bring about a 99 percent chance of two strangers being saved, though no two in particular (each particular stranger gets a very small chance of being saved).

- *Concentration v. Open Diffusion*: You can either pay $X to give one particular stranger a 99 percent chance of being saved or instead pay $X to bring about a 99 percent chance of at least two strangers being saved.

- *Concentration v. Risky Diffusion*: You can either pay $X to give one particular stranger a 99 percent chance of being saved or instead pay $X to bring about a 1/300 chance of saving 600 strangers.

- *Costless Conflict*: Three strangers face a deadly threat. You can do nothing, save one stranger's life at no cost to yourself, or save the other two at no cost to yourself. Tragically, you cannot save all three.

- *Costless No-Conflict*: Two strangers face a deadly threat. You can do nothing, save one stranger's life at no cost to yourself, or save both their lives at no cost to yourself.

- *Costless Rescue*: A stranger faces a deadly threat. You can either do nothing, allowing them to die, or you can, at no cost to yourself, save their life.

- *Costless v. Costly*: Two strangers face a deadly threat. You can do nothing, save one stranger's life at no cost to yourself, or save both their lives at great cost to yourself.

- *Costly Conflict*: Three strangers face a deadly threat. You can do nothing, save one stranger's life at great cost to yourself, or save the other two at the same great cost to yourself.

- *Costly No-Conflict*: Two strangers face a deadly threat. You can do nothing, save one stranger's life at great cost to yourself, or save both their lives at the same great cost to yourself.
- *Costly Rescue*: A stranger faces a deadly threat. You can either do nothing, allowing them to die, or you can, at great cost to yourself, save their life.
- *Dull*: While out for a hike in a country you have never been to before, you see on the map of your phone a red dot indicating that there is an emergency about 1000 miles away from you. You tap the dot for a brief description of the situation. It turns out that a boulder is hurtling toward stranger *B*. The remaining details are just like those in *Vivid*, except that there is no video making *B*'s plight especially salient to you. All you have is the relatively dull depiction, via the brief written description on your phone.
- *Far*: While out for a hike in a country you have never been to before, you see on the map of your phone a red dot indicating that there is an emergency about *1000 miles* away from you. You tap the dot for a brief description of the situation. It turns out that, on the other side of a tall brick wall, a boulder is hurtling toward stranger B. The remaining details are just like those in *Near*.
- *FarPlus*: While out for a hike in a country you have never been to before, you see on the map of your phone a red dot indicating that there is an emergency about 1000 miles away from you. You tap the dot for a brief description of the situation. There are 3000 boulders about to crush 3000 strangers, one boulder per stranger. As in *Injustice*, their plight is the

result of unjust institutions and social structures, though it is very rare for any of us to be able to help save those whose plights result from these structures. You realize that you can help. As in *Open Diffusion*, for $X you can tap a button on the screen of your phone that will give each of these 3000 strangers an independent 1/300 (times 99/100) chance of being saved so that there is a greater than 99 percent chance that at least one stranger or another will be saved (and a good chance that more than one will be saved). Many other people can similarly help these strangers, but you are certain none of them will.

- *Flight*: Two strangers are about to die. You have three alternatives. First, you can do nothing, letting both strangers die. Second, you can rescue in a way that will save one stranger and cause you to miss your nonrefundable international flight. Third, you can rescue in another way that will save both strangers, cause you to miss your flight, *and* muddy your clothes. (Suppose that, were you to save just one stranger, your motivation would be to avoid the combined cost of missing your flight and muddying your clothes—you're not willing to incur any more cost than that of a missed flight.)

- *Frequent Friend v. Strangers*: Once every minute for the indefinite future, you will be able to pay $3000 to save a different stranger from being crushed by a boulder. For the rest of your life, you will receive $3000 for every minute you stand on a large green button. This is the only way you can acquire money. There are no other ways of helping strangers—for example, you cannot ever donate to charities. Apart from taking breaks to do what you must in order to survive, you could spend the remainder of your life saving strangers from being crushed by boulders. You would not enjoy standing on the green button all day long, day after day. And, while standing on the green button, you would be incrementally missing out on things that make life worth living. *In addition*, on some number of occasions you will have the opportunity to pay $6000 to save a friend from being crushed by a boulder. (If there is more than one such occasion, it'll be a different friend each time; I assume you could in theory have very many friends.)

- *Frequent NearPlus*: Upon your arrival in a country you have never been to before, your trusty phone informs you that a series of accidents is about to occur. For the indefinite future, boulder upon boulder will threaten stranger upon stranger.

  Once every minute, you will see on the map of your phone a red dot indicating that there is an emergency about 10 feet away from you. On the other side of a tall brick wall, a boulder will be hurtling toward a stranger. Your phone will then display a live video of the stranger screaming in terror while trying to escape from the boulder. You will find it difficult to put their plight out of your mind. For $3000, you will be able to tap a button on the screen of your phone that will cause a large bulldozer to move in front of the boulder, bringing about a 99 percent chance of saving the stranger. No one else will be able to help the imperiled stranger.

  Three thousand dollars per minute adds up quickly (around $4.3 million per day!). Fortunately, for the rest of your life, you will receive $3000 for every minute you stand on a large green button. This is the only way you can acquire money. There are no other ways of helping strangers—for example, you cannot ever donate to charities. Apart from taking breaks to do what you must in order to survive, you could spend the remainder of your life saving strangers from being crushed by boulders. You would not enjoy standing on the green button all day long, day after day. And, while standing on the green button, you would be incrementally missing out on things that make life worth living. You are, however, able to switch off the boulder-emergency notifications on your phone. At any point, you can take a break or walk away from the rescue situation entirely (taking any money with you that you acquired from standing on the green button). Of course, either will mean letting more strangers die.

- *Frequent Stranger v. Strangers*: Once every minute for the indefinite future, you will be able to pay $3000 to save a different stranger from being crushed by a boulder. For the rest of your life, you will receive $3000 for every minute you stand on a large green button. This is the only way you can acquire money. There are no other ways of helping strangers—for example, you cannot ever donate to charities. Apart from taking breaks to do what you must in order to survive, you could spend the remainder of your life saving strangers from being crushed by boulders. You would not enjoy standing on the green button all day long, day after day. And, while standing on the green button, you would be incrementally missing out on things that make life worth living. *In addition*, on some number of occasions you will have the opportunity to pay $6000 to save a different stranger from being crushed by a boulder. That is, on these occasions, you have to decide whether to spend $6000 saving one *stranger* or saving two other *strangers* at $3000 each.

- *Friend*: While out for a hike in a country you have never been to before, you see on the map of your phone a red dot indicating that there is an emergency about 1000 miles away from you. You tap the dot for a brief description of the situation. It turns out that, on the other side of a tall brick wall, a boulder is hurtling toward your *friend*, *A*, who is stuck in the boulder's path. You cannot reach *A* yourself but realize that, for X, you can save *A*'s life using your phone. Many other people can similarly help *A*, but you are certain none of them will. As it happens, you'd never see *A* again anyway as they're about to move to a remote monastery where they'd stay for the rest of their life. Also, you recently accidentally ingested an antidepressant that makes the psychological costs of letting *A* die roughly equivalent to the psychological costs of letting a stranger die.

- *Friend v. Strangers*: You can either pay X to save your friend, *A*, or instead pay X to save two strangers.

- *Hand*: One hundred strangers are about to die, and another stranger, *Z*, is about to lose their finger. You can do nothing, save just the lives of the 100 strangers at the cost of losing your non-dominant hand, or save the 100 and *Z*'s finger at the cost of losing your non-dominant hand *and* stubbing your toe. (Suppose that, were you to save just the lives of the 100 strangers, your motivation would be to avoid the combined cost of losing your hand and stubbing your toe—you're not willing to incur any more cost than that of a lost hand.)

- *Harmful Conflict*: You face a severe harm. You can do nothing, save yourself in a way that moderately harms one stranger, or save yourself in another way that equally harms each of two other strangers.

- *Injustice*: While out for a hike in a country you have never been to before, you see on the map of your phone a red dot indicating that there is an emergency about 1000 miles away from you. You tap the dot for a brief description of the situation. It turns out that a boulder is hurtling toward stranger *A*, who is stuck in the boulder's path. *A*'s plight is the result of unjust institutions and social structures: *A* is one of many workers living in extreme poverty who, to provide for themselves and their families, have to take a risky route to and from work each day. Along this route, falling boulders regularly kill workers. Although we could collectively reform the unjust social structures and thereby prevent these tragic deaths, it is very rare that any of us could save an individual worker from a falling boulder (it is as rare as cases like *Pond*). However, you realize that you are able to save *A*'s life using your phone. For $X you can tap a button on the screen of your phone that causes a large bulldozer to move in front of the boulder, saving *A* without doing any damage to the bulldozer. Many other people can similarly help *A*, but you are certain none of them will.

- *Many*: While out for a hike in a country you have never been to before, you see on the map of your phone a red dot indicating that there is an emergency about 1000 miles away from you. You tap the dot for a brief description of the situation. It turns out that a boulder is hurtling toward stranger *B*. The remaining details are just like those in *Alone*, except that many other people can similarly help B, and you are certain none of them will.

- *Near*: While out for a hike in a country you have never been to before, you see on the map of your phone a red dot indicating that there is an emergency about *10 feet* away from you. You tap the dot for a brief description of the situation. It turns out that, on the other side of a tall brick wall, a boulder is hurtling toward stranger *A*, who is stuck in the boulder's path. You cannot reach *A* yourself but realize that you are able to save *A*'s life using your phone. For $X you can tap a button on the screen of your phone that causes a large bulldozer to move in front of the boulder, saving *A* without doing any damage to the bulldozer. Many other people can similarly help *A*, but you are certain none of them will.
- *NearPlus*: While out for a hike in a country you have never been to before, you see on the map of your phone a red dot indicating that there is an emergency about 10 feet away from you. You tap the dot for a brief description of the situation. It turns out that, on the other side of a tall brick wall, a boulder is hurtling toward stranger *A*. Immediately after you read this, your phone displays a live video of *A* screaming in terror while trying to escape from the boulder. You find it difficult to put their plight out of your mind. You realize that you can save *A*'s life using your phone. For $X you can tap a button on the screen of your phone that will cause a large bulldozer to move in front of the boulder,

bringing about a 99 percent chance of saving *A*. No one else can help *A*.

- *Near v. Far*: While out for a hike in a country you have never been to before, you see on the map of your phone two red dots indicating that there are two emergencies. You tap the dots for brief descriptions of the situations. About 10 feet away, on the other side of a tall brick wall, a boulder is hurtling toward stranger *A* (who is stuck in the boulder's path), and about 1000 miles farther away, another boulder is hurtling toward strangers *B* and *C* (who are stuck in this other boulder's path). You cannot reach any of these strangers yourself but realize that, using your phone, you are able to either save *A* for $X or instead save *B* and *C* for $X. You cannot save all three. Many other people can similarly help, but you are certain none of them will.

- *NearPlus v. FarPlus*: You can either pay $X to give one particular stranger (in a situation like *NearPlus*) a 99 percent chance of being saved or instead pay $X to bring about a 99 percent chance of at least two strangers (in a situation like *FarPlus*) being saved.

- *Open Diffusion*: As in *Closed Diffusion*, except now there are 10 times as many strangers, boulders, and bulldozers (3000 of each), and paying $X will not certainly activate one or another of the bulldozers. Instead, paying $X will give *each* particular bulldozer an independent 1/300 chance of being activated, and, if activated, a bulldozer will move into the path of its corresponding boulder, bringing about a 99 percent chance of stopping it. While each particular stranger would thus get a 1/300 (times 99/100) chance of being saved, there is a chance no one would be saved. But there is a greater than 99 percent chance that *at least* one stranger or another would be saved (and a good chance that more than one would be saved).

- *Pond*: You are walking past a shallow pond and see a stranger drowning in it. You can safely wade in and pull the stranger out, but this will mean ruining your new clothes. If you do not save the stranger, they will die.
- *Pond v. Charity*: You are walking past a shallow pond and see a stranger drowning in it. You can safely wade in and pull the stranger out, but this will mean losing $6000 you could donate to a malaria charity that saves on average one life for every $3000 it receives (if you wade in with the money, it will be destroyed by the dirty water, and if you try to leave it on the side of the pond, the wind will blow it in). You can donate this money to the charity only if you let the stranger drown.
- *Rare/Frequent NearPlus*: You are in *Frequent NearPlus*, but in addition to indicating every minute that yet another boulder is threatening yet another stranger, your trusty phone will very rarely indicate that a small iron meteorite is threatening a lone stranger 10 feet away on the other side of a tall brick wall. As before, your phone will then display a live video of the stranger, and you will find it difficult to put their plight out of your mind. You will realize that you are able to save their life. If you stand on a red button for a minute, this will bring about a 99 percent chance that a large underground magnet—located a few miles away—will divert the meteorite into an empty field, saving the stranger.

No one else can help the lone stranger. During the minute that you are able to save a stranger from a meteorite by standing on the red button, you will be unable to use your phone to save a stranger from a boulder. You cannot stand on both the red button and the green button at the same time—so you can't collect $3000 from the green button while you're on the red button. But if you do stand on the green button during the minute that you could have saved someone from a meteorite by standing on the red button, you cannot use the money obtained from the green button during that minute to later save a stranger from a boulder (during that minute, standing on the green button would get you $3000 in cash rather than the usual electronic money, and you can't use cash on your phone to save a stranger from a boulder). While you are able to switch off the very frequent boulder-emergency notifications on your phone, you are unable to switch off the rare meteorite-emergency notifications.

- *Risky Diffusion*: As in *Closed Diffusion*, except now a single boulder is about to crush all 300 strangers, who are together stuck in its path. You can pay $X to bring about a 1/300 chance that a bulldozer will block the boulder, saving all these strangers. While each particular stranger would get a 1/300 chance of being saved, there is a very good (299/300) chance *no one* would be saved.

- *Stranger*: While out for a hike in a country you have never been to before, you see on the map of your phone a red dot indicating that there is an emergency about 1000 miles away from you. It turns out that, on the other side of a tall brick wall, a boulder is hurtling toward a *stranger, B*. The remaining details are just like those in *Friend*.

- *10 Plus Conflict*: You can do nothing; press a red button, thereby saving the lives of 10 strangers and the life of stranger X; or press a green button, thereby saving the lives of these same 10 strangers and the lives of strangers Y and Z. Pressing either button will also cause you to drop into a fiery pit and die.

- *Vivid*: While out for a hike in a country you have never been to before, you see on the map of your phone a red dot indicating that there is an emergency about 1000 miles away from you. You tap the dot for a brief description of the situation. It turns out that a boulder is hurtling toward stranger A, who is stuck in the boulder's path. Immediately after you read this, your phone displays a live video of A screaming in terror while trying to escape from the boulder. You find it difficult to put their plight out of your mind. You realize that you can save A's life using your phone. For $\$X$ you can tap a button on the screen of your phone that causes a large bulldozer to move in front of the boulder, saving A without doing any damage to the bulldozer. Many other people can similarly help A, but you are certain none of them will.

- *Vivid Plus Near*: While out for a hike in a country you have never been to before, you see on the map of your phone a red dot indicating that there is an emergency about *10 feet* away from you. You tap the dot for a brief description of the situation. It turns out that, on the other side of a tall brick wall, a boulder is hurtling toward stranger A, who is stuck in the boulder's path. The remaining details are just like those in *Vivid*.

- *Vivid v. Dull*: While out for a hike in a country you have never been to before, you see on the map of your phone two red dots indicating that there are two emergencies. You tap the dots for brief descriptions of the situations. About 1000 miles away, a boulder is hurtling toward stranger *A* (who is stuck in the boulder's path), and about 1000 miles away in the opposite direction, another boulder is hurtling toward strangers *B* and *C* (who are stuck in this other boulder's path). *A*'s plight is especially salient to you (because it is vividly depicted, as in *Vivid*) but the plights of *B* and *C* are not (because they are dully depicted, as in *Dull*). You realize that, using your phone, you can either save *A* for $X or instead save *B* and *C* for $X. You cannot save all three. Many other people can similarly help, but you are certain none of them will.

- *Your Life v. Stranger's Legs*: You can do nothing; press a red button, thereby saving stranger *A*'s legs; or press a green button, thereby saving stranger *A*'s legs and stranger *B*'s finger. Pressing either button will also cause you to drop into a fiery pit and die.

BIBLIOGRAPHY

Anderson, Elizabeth. 1999. "What is the Point of Equality?" *Ethics* 109: 287–337.

Anscombe, Elizabeth. 1967. "Who Is Wronged?" *Oxford Review* 5: 16–17.

Appiah, Kwame. 2008. *Experiments in Ethics*. Cambridge, MA: Harvard University Press.

Arneson, Richard. 2000. "Luck Egalitarianism and Prioritarianism." *Ethics* 110: 339–349.

Arneson, Richard. 2003a. "The Smart Theory of Moral Responsibility and Desert." In *Desert and Justice*, ed. Serena Olsaretti, Oxford: Oxford University Press, pp. 233–258.

Arneson, Richard. 2003b. "Consequentialism vs. Special-Ties Partiality." *The Monist* 86: 382–401.

Arneson, Richard. 2004. "Moral Limits on the Demands of Beneficence?" In *The Ethics of Assistance: Morality and the Distant Needy*, ed. Deen Chatterjee, Cambridge: Cambridge University Press, pp. 33–58.

Arneson, Richard. 2020. "Against Patriotism and National Partiality." In *Handbook of Patriotism*, ed. Mitja Sardoč, Cham: Springer, pp. 429–450.

Arpaly, Nomy. 2003. *Unprincipled Virtue: An Inquiry into Moral Agency*. Oxford: Oxford University Press.

Ashford, Elizabeth. 2018. "Severe Poverty as an Unjust Emergency." In *The Ethics of Giving: Philosophers' Perspectives on Philanthropy*, ed. Paul Woodruff, New York: Oxford University Press, pp. 103–148.

Askell, Amanda. 2019. "Evidence Neutrality and the Moral Value of Information." In *Effective Altruism: Philosophical Issues*, eds. Hilary Greaves and Theron Pummer, Oxford: Oxford University Press, pp. 37–52.

Bader, Ralf. 2019. "Agent-Relative Prerogatives and Suboptimal Beneficence." *Oxford Studies in Normative Ethics* 9: 223–250.

Barnes, Elizabeth. 2016. *The Minority Body: A Theory of Disability*. Oxford: Oxford University Press.

Barry, Christian, and Holly Lawford-Smith. 2019. "On Satisfying Duties to Assist." In *Effective Altruism: Philosophical Issues*, eds. Hilary Greaves and Theron Pummer, Oxford: Oxford University Press, pp. 150–165.

Barry, Christian, and Seth Lazar. 2022. "Supererogation and Optimisation." *Australasian Journal of Philosophy*. doi:10.1080/00048402.2022.2074066

Barry, Christian, and Gerhard Øverland. 2013. "How Much for the Child?" *Ethical Theory and Moral Practice* 16: 189–204.

Barry, Christian, and Gerhard Øverland. 2016. *Responding to Global Poverty: Harm, Responsibility, and Agency*. Cambridge: Cambridge University Press.

Bazargan-Forward, Saba. 2018. "Vesting Agent-Relative Permissions in a Proxy." *Law and Philosophy* 37: 671–695.

Bell, Macalester. 2013. "The Standing to Blame: A Critique." In *Blame: Its Nature and Norms*, eds. Justin Coates and Neal Tognazzini, New York: Oxford University Press, pp. 263–281.

Berg, Amy. 2018. "Effective Altruism: How Big Should the Tent Be?" *Public Affairs Quarterly* 32: 269–287.

Berkey, Brian. 2018. "The Institutional Critique of Effective Altruism." *Utilitas* 30: 143–171.

Berkey, Brian. 2020. "Effectiveness and Demandingness." *Utilitas* 32: 368–381.

Berkey, Brian. 2021. "The Philosophical Core of Effective Altruism." *Journal of Social Philosophy* 52: 92–113.

Bloom, Paul. 2016. *Against Empathy: The Case for Rational Compassion*. New York: Ecco.

Bowen, Joseph. unpublished. "Enforcement and Supererogation."

Bradley, Ben. 2009. "Saving People and Flipping Coins." *Journal of Ethics and Social Philosophy* 3: 1–13.

Bradley, Ben. 2012. "Doing Away with Harm." *Philosophy and Phenomenological Research* 85: 390–412.

Brink, David. 2001. "Impartiality and Associative Duties." *Utilitas* 13: 152–172.

Brink, David. 2014. "Principles and Intuitions in Ethics: Historical and Contemporary Perspectives." *Ethics* 124: 665–694.

Brink, David. 2020. "Consequentialism, the Separateness of Persons, and Aggregation." In *The Oxford Handbook of Consequentialism*, ed. Douglas Portmore, New York: Oxford University Press, pp. 378–400.

Broome, John. 1990. "Fairness." *Proceedings of the Aristotelian Society* 91: 87–101.

Buchak, Lara. 2013. *Risk and Rationality*. Oxford: Oxford University Press.

Budolfson, Mark. 2019. "The Inefficacy Objection to Consequentialism and the Problem with the Expected Consequences Response." *Philosophical Studies* 176: 1711–1724.

Budolfson, Mark, and Dean Spears. 2019. "The Hidden Zero Problem: Effective Altruism and Barriers to marginal Impact." In *Effective Altruism: Philosophical Issues*, eds. Hilary Greaves and Theron Pummer, Oxford: Oxford University Press, pp. 184–201.

Burri, Susanne. 2020. "Why Moral Theorizing Needs Real Cases: The Redirection of V-Weapons During the Second World War." *Journal of Political Philosophy* 28: 247–269.

Burum, Bethany, Martin Nowak, and Moshe Hoffman. 2020. "An Evolutionary Explanation for Ineffective Altruism." *Nature Human Behaviour* 4: 1245–1257.

Buss, Sarah. 2006. "Needs (Someone Else's), Projects (My Own), and Reasons." *Journal of Philosophy* 103: 373–402.

Bykvist, Krister. 2007. "Violations of Normative Invariance: Some Thoughts on Shifty Oughts." *Theoria* 73: 98–120.

Casal, Paula. 2007. "Why Sufficiency Is Not Enough." *Ethics* 117: 296–326.

Caviola, Lucius, and Stefan Schubert. unpublished. "Is it Obligatory to Donate Effectively? Judgments about the Wrongness of Donating Ineffectively."

Caviola, Lucius, Stefan Schubert, and Joshua Greene. 2021. "The Psychology of (In)Effective Altruism." *Trends in Cognitive Sciences* 25: 596–607.

Caviola, Lucius, Stefan Schubert, and Jason Nemirow. 2020. "The Many Obstacles to Effective Giving." *Judgement and Decision Making* 15: 159–172.

Chang, Ruth. 2002. "The Possibility of Parity." *Ethics* 112: 659–688.

Chappell, Richard Yetter. 2016. "Against 'Saving Lives': Equal Concern and Differential Impact." *Bioethics* 30: 159–164.

Chappell, Richard Yetter. 2019. "Overriding Virtue." In *Effective Altruism: Philosophical Issues*, eds. Hilary Greaves and Theron Pummer, Oxford: Oxford University Press, pp. 218–226.

Chappell, Sophie Grace. 2015. *Intuition, Theory, and Anti-Theory in Ethics.* Oxford: Oxford University Press.

Chisholm, R. M. 1963. "Contrary-to-Duty Imperatives and Deontic Logic." *Analysis* 24: 33–36.

Clark, Matthew, and Theron Pummer. 2019. "Each-We Dilemmas and Effective Altruism." *Journal of Practical Ethics* 7: 24–32.

Collins, Stephanie. 2019. "Beyond Individualism." In *Effective Altruism: Philosophical Issues*, eds. Hilary Greaves and Theron Pummer, Oxford: Oxford University Press, pp. 202–217.

Comesaña, Juan. 2015. "Normative Requirements and Contrary-to-Duty Obligations." *Journal of Philosophy* 112: 600–626.

Cordelli, Chiara. 2018. "Prospective Duties and the Demands of Beneficence." *Ethics* 128: 373–401.

Côté, Nicolas, and Bastian Steuwer. 2022. "Better Vaguely Right than Precisely Wrong in Effective Altruism: The Problem of Marginalism." *Economics and Philosophy*. doi:10.1017/S0266267122000062

Crisp, Roger. 2015. *The Cosmos of Duty: Henry Sidgwick's Methods of Ethics.* Oxford: Oxford University Press.

Crisp, Roger. 2018. "Against Partiality." *The Lindley Lecture.* University of Kansas.

Crisp, Roger, and Theron Pummer. 2020. "Effective Justice." *Journal of Moral Philosophy* 17: 398–415.

Cullity, Garrett. 2004. *The Moral Demands of Affluence.* Oxford: Oxford University Press.

Dancy, Jonathan. 2004. *Ethics without Principles*. Oxford: Oxford University Press.

Darwall, Stephen. 2010. "But It Would Be Wrong." *Social Philosophy and Policy* 27: 135–157.

Darwall, Stephen. 2013. *Morality, Authority, and Law: Essays in Second-Personal Ethics*. Oxford: Oxford University Press.

Davis, Jeremy. 2021. "Scope Restrictions, National Partiality, and War." *Journal of Ethics and Social Philosophy* 20: 144–167.

Deaton, Angus. 2013. *The Great Escape: Health, Wealth, and the Origins of Inequality*. Princeton: Princeton University Press.

DeGrazia, David. 1996. *Taking Animals Seriously: Mental Life and Moral Status*. Cambridge: Cambridge University Press.

Dietz, Alexander. 2019. "Effective Altruism and Collective Obligations." *Utilitas* 31: 106–115.

Doggett, Tyler. 2013. "Saving the Few." *Nous* 47: 302–315.

Dougherty, Tom. 2014. "Vague Value." *Philosophy and Phenomenological Research* 89: 352–372.

Dougherty, Tom. 2017. "Altruism and Ambition in the Dynamic Moral Life." *Australasian Journal of Philosophy* 95: 716–729.

Driver, Julia. 1992. "The Suberogatory." *Australasian Journal of Philosophy* 70: 286–295.

Ellis, Anthony. 1992. "Deontology, Incommensurability and the Arbitrary." *Philosophy and Phenomenological Research* 52: 855–875.

Elster, Jakob. 2011. "How Outlandish Can Imaginary Cases Be?" *Journal of Applied Philosophy* 28: 241–258.

Fabre, Cécile. 2002. "Good Samaritanism: A Matter of Justice." *Critical Review of International Social and Political Philosophy* 5: 128–144.

Fabre, Cécile. 2012. *Cosmopolitan War*. Oxford: Oxford University Press.

Feinberg, Joel. 1984. *The Moral Limits of the Criminal Law. Volume 1: Harm to Others*. New York: Oxford University Press.

Ferguson, Benjamin, and Sebastian Köhler. 2020. "Betterness of Permissibility." *Philosophical Studies* 177: 2451–2469.

Fischer, Jessica. unpublished. "On Doing Less Good."

Forrester, James. 1984. "Gentle Murder, or the Adverbial Samaritan." *Journal of Philosophy* 81: 193–197.

Frick, Johann. 2015. "Contractualism and Social Risk." *Philosophy and Public Affairs* 43: 175–223.

Frick, Johann. unpublished. "Dilemmas, Luck, and the Two Faces of Morality."

Fried, Barbara. 2004. "Left-Libertarianism: A Review Essay." *Philosophy and Public Affairs* 32: 66–92.

Fried, Barbara. 2012. "What 'Does' Matter? The Case for Killing the Trolley Problem (or Letting It Die)." *Philosophical Quarterly* 62: 505–529.

Fried, Charles, and Derek Parfit. 1979. "Correspondence." *Philosophy and Public Affairs* 8: 393–397.

Frowe, Helen. 2019. "If You'll Be My Bodyguard: Agreements to Save and the Duty to Minimize Harm." *Ethics* 129: 204–229.

Frowe, Helen. 2021. "The Limited Use View and the Duty to Save." *Oxford Studies in Political Philosophy* 7: 66–99.

Gabriel, Iason, and Brian McElwee. 2019. "Effective Altruism, Global Poverty, and Systemic Change." In *Effective Altruism: Philosophical Issues*, eds. Hilary Greaves and Theron Pummer, Oxford: Oxford University Press, pp. 99–114.

Gert, Joshua. 2003. "Requiring and Justifying: Two Dimensions of Normative Strength." *Erkenntnis* 59: 5–36.

Gert, Joshua. 2016. "The Distinction between Justifying and Requiring: Nothing to Fear." In *Weighing Reasons*, eds. Errol Lord and Barry Maguire, Oxford: Oxford University Press, pp. 157–172.

Gibbard, Allan. 1990. *Wise Choices, Apt Feelings: A Theory of Normative Judgement*. Oxford: Oxford University Press.

Glover, Jonathan. 1977. *Causing Death and Saving Lives*. New York: Penguin.

Gomberg, Paul. 1990. "Patriotism Is Like Racism." *Ethics* 101: 144–150.

Goodin, Robert. 1985. *Protecting the Vulnerable: A Reanalysis of Our Social Responsibilities*. Chicago: Chicago University Press.

Gordon-Solmon, Kerah. 2019. "Should Contractualists Decompose?" *Philosophy and Public Affairs* 47: 259–287.

Gordon-Solmon, Kerah. unpublished. "Between All and Nothing: Or, Defending the Impermissible."

Greaves, Hilary. 2016. "Cluelessness." *Proceedings of the Aristotelian Society* 116: 311–339.

Greenspan, Patricia. 2010. "Making Room for Options: Moral Reasons, Imperfect Duties, and Choice." *Social Philosophy and Policy* 27: 181–205.

Hájek, Alan. 2019. "Interpretations of Probability." In *The Stanford Encyclopedia of Philosophy*, ed. Edward Zalta. https://plato.stanford.edu/entries/probability-interpret/

Hanser, Matthew. 2014. "Imperfect Aiding." In *The Cambridge Companion of Life and Death*, ed. Steven Luper, Cambridge: Cambridge University Press, pp. 300–315.

Hansson, Bengt. 1969. "An Analysis of Some Deontic Logics." *Nous* 3: 373–398.

Hare, Caspar. 2012. "Obligations to Merely Statistical People." *Journal of Philosophy* 109: 378–390.

Harman, Elizabeth. 2009. "Harming as Causing Harm." In *Harming Future Persons: Ethics, Genetics and the Nonidentity Problem*, eds. Melinda Roberts and David Wasserman, Dordrecht: Springer, pp. 137–154.

Harman, Elizabeth. 2015. "Is It Reasonable to 'Rely on Intuitions' in Ethics?" In *The Norton Introduction to Philosophy*, eds. Alex Byrne, Joshua Cohen, Gideon Rosen, and Seana Shiffrin, New York: Norton, pp. 895–903.

Harris, John. 1995. "Double Jeopardy and the Veil of Ignorance: A Reply." *Journal of Medical Ethics* 21: 151–157.

Haydar, Bashshar, and Gerhard Øverland. 2019. "Hypocrisy, Poverty Alleviation, and Two Types of Emergencies." *Journal of Ethics* 23: 3–17.

Herman, Barbara. 2012. "Being Helped and Being Grateful: Imperfect Duties, the Ethics of Possession, and the Unity of Morality." *Journal of Philosophy* 109: 391–411.

Hill, Thomas E., Jr. 2002. *Human Welfare and Moral Worth: Kantian Perspectives*. Oxford: Oxford University Press.

Hirose, Iwao. 2014. *Moral Aggregation*. Oxford: Oxford University Press.

Hohfeld, Wesley Newcomb. 1913. "Some Fundamental Legal Conceptions as Applied in Judicial Reasoning." *The Yale Law Journal* 23: 16–59.

Hooker, Brad. 2000. *Ideal Code, Real World: A Rule-Consequentialist Theory of Morality*. Oxford: Oxford University Press.

Hooker, Brad. 2009. "The Demandingness Objection." In *The Problem of Moral Demandingness: New Philosophical Essays*, ed. Timothy Chappell, London: Palgrave Macmillan, pp. 148–162.

Horgan, Terry, and Mark Timmons. 2010. "Untying a Knot from the Inside Out: Reflections on the 'Paradox' of Supererogation." *Social Philosophy and Policy* 27: 29–63.

Horton, Joe. 2017a. "The All or Nothing Problem." *Journal of Philosophy* 114: 94–104.

Horton, Joe. 2017b. "Aggregation, Complaints, and Risk." *Philosophy and Public Affairs* 45: 54–81.

Horton, Joe. 2021. "Partial Aggregation in Ethics." *Philosophy Compass* 16: 1–12.

Huemer, Michael. 2005. *Ethical Intuitionism*. New York: Palgrave Macmillan.

Hurka, Thomas. 1990. "Two Kinds of Satisficing." *Philosophical Studies* 59: 107–111.

Hurka, Thomas. 1997. "The Justification of National Partiality." In *The Morality of Nationalism*, ed. Robert McKim and Jeff McMahan, New York: Oxford University Press, pp. 139–157.

Hurka, Thomas, and Esther Shubert. 2012. "Permissions to Do Less Than Best: A Moving Band." *Oxford Studies in Normative Ethics* 2: 1–27.

Hurka, Thomas, and Evangeline Tsagarakis. 2021. "More Supererogatory." In *Principles and Persons: The Legacy of Derek Parfit*, eds. Jeff McMahan, Tim Campbell, James Goodrich, and Ketan Ramakrishnan, Oxford: Oxford University Press, pp. 463–477.

Jackson, Frank. 1985. "On the Semantics and Logic of Obligation." *Mind* 94: 177–195.

Jeske, Diane. 1998. "Families, Friends, and Special Obligations." *Canadian Journal of Philosophy* 28: 527–555.

Kagan, Shelly. 1988. "The Additive Fallacy." *Ethics* 99: 5–31.

Kagan, Shelly. 1989. *The Limits of Morality*. Oxford: Oxford University Press.

Kagan, Shelly. 1998. *Normative Ethics*. Boulder: Westview Press.

Kagan, Shelly. 2001. "Thinking about Cases." *Social Philosophy and Policy* 18: 44–63.

Kagan, Shelly. 2011. "Do I Make a Difference?" *Philosophy and Public Affairs* 39: 105–141.

Kagan, Shelly. 2019. *How to Count Animals, More or Less*. Oxford: Oxford University Press.

Kamm, Frances. 1983. "Killing and Letting Die: Methodological and Substantive Issues." *Pacific Philosophical Quarterly* 64: 297–312.

Kamm, Frances. 1985. "Supererogation and Obligation." *Journal of Philosophy* 82: 118–138.

Kamm, Frances. 1992. "Non-Consequentialism, the Person as an End-in-Itself, and the Significance of Status." *Philosophy and Public Affairs* 21: 354–389.

Kamm, Frances. 1993. *Morality, Mortality. Volume I: Death and Whom to Save from It*. New York: Oxford University Press.

Kamm, Frances. 1996. *Morality, Mortality. Volume II: Rights, Duties, and Status*. New York: Oxford University Press.

Kamm, Frances. 2000. "Does Distance Matter Morally to the Duty to Rescue?" *Law and Philosophy* 19: 655–681.

Kamm, Frances. 2005. "Aggregation and Two Moral Methods." *Utilitas* 17: 1–23.

Kamm, Frances. 2007. *Intricate Ethics: Rights, Responsibilities, and Permissible Harm*. New York: Oxford University Press.

Kamm, Frances. 2009. "Aggregation, Allocating Scarce Resources, and the Disabled." *Social Philosophy and Policy* 26: 148–197.

Kamm, Frances. 2013. *Bioethical Prescriptions: To Create, End, Choose, and Improve Lives*. New York: Oxford University Press.

Kamm, Frances. 2021. "Duties That Become Supererogatory or Forbidden?" In *Principles and Persons: The Legacy of Derek Parfit*, eds. Jeff McMahan, Tim Campbell, James Goodrich, and Ketan Ramakrishnan, Oxford: Oxford University Press, pp. 441–462.

Kavka, Gregory. 1979. "The Numbers Should Count." *Philosophical Studies* 36: 285–294.

Keller, Simon. 2013. *Partiality*. Princeton: Princeton University Press.

Kolodny, Niko. 2010. "Which Relationships Justify Partiality? The Case of Parents and Children." *Philosophy and Public Affairs* 38: 37–75.

Korsgaard, Christine. 2018. *Fellow Creatures: Our Obligations to the Other Animals*. Oxford: Oxford University Press.

Kratzer, Angelika. 2012. *Modals and Conditionals: New and Revised Perspectives*. Oxford: Oxford University Press.

Kumar, Rahul. 2011. "Contractualism on the Shoal of Aggregation." In *Reasons and Recognition: Essays on the Philosophy of T. M. Scanlon*, eds. R. Jay Wallace, Rahul Kumar, and Samuel Freeman, New York: Oxford University Press, pp. 129–154.

Kumar, Rahul. unpublished. "Saving Lives and Statistical Deaths."

Lamont, Julian, and Christi Favor. 2017. "Distributive Justice." In *The Stanford Encyclopedia of Philosophy*, ed. Edward Zalta. https://plato.stanford.edu/entries/justice-distributive/

Lange, Benjamin. 2020. "Other-Sacrificing Options." *Philosophy and Phenomenological Research* 101: 612–629.

Lazar, Seth. 2019. "Accommodating Options." *Pacific Philosophical Quarterly* 100: 233–255.

Lechterman, Theodore. 2021. *The Tyranny of Generosity: Why Philanthropy Corrupts Our Politics and How We Can Fix It*. New York: Oxford University Press.

Lenman, James. 2000. "Consequentialism and Cluelessness." *Philosophy and Public Affairs* 29: 342–370.

Liao, S. Matthew. 2008. "Who Is Afraid of Numbers?" *Utilitas* 20: 447–461.

Liao, S. Matthew. 2012. "Intentions and Moral Permissibility: The Case of Acting Permissibly with Bad Intentions." *Law and Philosophy* 31: 703–724.

Lippert-Rasmussen, Kasper. 2019. "Barry and Øverland on Singer and Assistance-Based Duties." *Ethics and Global Politics* 12: 15–23.

Little, Margaret, and Coleen Macnamara. 2017. "For Better or Worse: Commendatory Reasons and Latitude." *Oxford Studies in Normative Ethics* 7: 138–160.

MacAskill, William. 2015. *Doing Good Better: How Effective Altruism Can Help You Help Others, Do Work That Matters, and Make Smarter Choices about Giving Back*. New York: Penguin Random House.

MacAskill, William. 2019a. "The Definition of Effective Altruism." In *Effective Altruism: Philosophical Issues*, eds. Hilary Greaves and Theron Pummer, Oxford: Oxford University Press, pp. 10–28.

MacAskill, William. 2019b. "Aid Scepticism and Effective Altruism." *Journal of Practical Ethics* 7: 49–60.

MacAskill, William. forthcoming. *What We Owe The Future: A Million-Year View*. New York: Basic Books.

MacAskill, William, Andreas Mogensen, and Toby Ord. 2018. "Giving Isn't Demanding." In *The Ethics of Giving: Philosophers' Perspectives on Philanthropy*, ed. Paul Woodruff, New York: Oxford University Press, pp. 178–203.

MacAskill, William, and Theron Pummer. 2020. "Effective Altruism." In *International Encyclopedia of Ethics*. https://doi.org/10.1002/978144 4367072.wbiee883

Malm, H. M. 1995. "Liberalism, Bad Samaritan Law, and Legal Paternalism." *Ethics* 106: 4–31.

Markovits, Julia. 2012. "Saints, Heroes, Sages, and Villains." *Philosophical Studies* 158: 289–311.

Mason, Elinor. 2019. *Ways to Be Blameworthy: Rightness, Wrongness, and Responsibility*. Oxford: Oxford University Press.

Massoud, Amy. 2016. "Moral Worth and Supererogation." *Ethics* 126: 690–710.

McElwee, Brian. 2016. "What Is Demandingness?" In *The Limits of Moral Obligation: Moral Demandingness and Ought Implies Can*, eds. M. van Ackeren and M. Kühler, Abingdon: Routledge, pp. 19–35.

McElwee, Brian. 2017. "Demandingness Objections in Ethics." *Philosophical Quarterly* 67: 84–105.

McGrath, Sarah. 2019. *Moral Knowledge*. Oxford: Oxford University Press.

McMahan, Jeff. 2000. "Moral Intuition." In *Blackwell Guide to Ethical Theory*, ed. Hugh LaFollette, Oxford: Blackwell, pp. 92–110.

McMahan, Jeff. 2018. "Doing Good and Doing the Best." In *The Ethics of Giving: Philosophers' Perspectives on Philanthropy*, ed. Paul Woodruff, New York: Oxford University Press, pp. 78–102.

McNamara, Paul. 2019. "Deontic Logic." In *The Stanford Encyclopedia of Philosophy*, ed. Edward Zalta. https://plato.stanford.edu/archives/sum2 019/entries/logic-deontic/

Miller, David. 2020. "The Nature and Limits of the Duty of Rescue." *Journal of Moral Philosophy* 17: 320–341.

Mogensen, Andreas. 2019. "The Callousness Objection." In *Effective Altruism: Philosophical Issues*, eds. Hilary Greaves and Theron Pummer, Oxford: Oxford University Press, pp. 227–243.

Mogensen, Andreas. 2021. "Maximal Cluelessness." *Philosophical Quarterly* 71: 141–162.

Monton, Bradley. 2019. "How to Avoid Maximizing Expected Utility." *Philosophers' Imprint* 19: 1–25.

Mulgan, Tim. 1993. "Slote's Satisficing Consequentialism." *Ratio* 6: 121–134.

Muñoz, Daniel. 2021. "Three Paradoxes of Supererogation." *Nous* 55: 699–716.

Muñoz, Daniel, and Theron Pummer. 2022. "Supererogation and Conditional Obligation." *Philosophical Studies* 179: 1429–1443. https://doi.org/ 10.1007/s11098-021-01724-y

Munoz-Dardé, Véronique. 2005. "The Distribution of Numbers and the Comprehensiveness of Reasons." *Proceedings of the Aristotelean Society* 105: 191–217.

Murphy, Liam. 1993. "The Demands of Beneficence." *Philosophy and Public Affairs* 22: 267–292.

Murphy, Liam, and Thomas Nagel. 2002. *The Myth of Ownership: Taxes and Justice*. New York: Oxford University Press.

Nefsky, Julia. 2019. "Collective Harm and the Inefficacy Problem." *Philosophy Compass* 14: e12587.

Nelkin, Dana. 2016. "Difficulty and Degrees of Moral Praiseworthiness and Blameworthiness." *Nous* 50: 356–378.

Nelkin, Dana. 2022. "How Much to Blame? An Asymmetry in the Norms of Self-Blame and Other Blame." In *Self-Blame and Moral Responsibility*, ed. Andreas Brekke Carlsson, Cambridge: Cambridge University Press, pp. 97–116.

Noggle, Robert. 2009. "Give Till It Hurts? Beneficence, Imperfect Duties, and a Moderate Response to the Aid Question." *Journal of Social Philosophy* 40: 1–16.

Nozick, Robert. 1974. *Anarchy, State, and Utopia*. New York: Basic Books.

Ord, Toby. 2019. "The Moral Imperative Toward Cost-Effectiveness in Global Health." In *Effective Altruism: Philosophical Issues*, eds. Hilary Greaves and Theron Pummer, Oxford: Oxford University Press, pp. 29–36.

Ord, Toby. 2020. *The Precipice: Existential Risk and the Future of Humanity*. New York: Hachette.

Otsuka, Michael. 2003. *Libertarianism without Inequality*. Oxford: Oxford University Press.

Otsuka, Michael. 2006. "Saving Lives, Moral Theory, and the Claims of Individuals." *Philosophy and Public Affairs* 34: 109–135.

Otsuka, Michael. 2015. "Risking Life and Limb: How to Discount Harms by Their Improbability." In *Identified versus Statistical Lives: An Interdisciplinary Perspective*, eds. Glenn Cohen, Norman Daniels, and Nir Eyal, New York: Oxford University Press, pp. 77–93.

Parfit, Derek. 1978. "Innumerate Ethics." *Philosophy and Public Affairs* 7: 285–301.

Parfit, Derek. 1982. "Future Generations: Further Problems." *Philosophy and Public Affairs* 11: 113–172.

Parfit, Derek. 1997. "Equality and Priority." *Ratio* 10: 202–221.

Parfit, Derek. 2003. "Justifiability to Each Person." *Ratio* 16: 368–390.

Parfit, Derek. 2011. *On What Matters: Volume 1*. Oxford: Oxford University Press.

Pettit, Philip. 1997. "Love and Its Place in Moral Discourse." In *Love Analyzed*, ed. Roger Lamb, Boulder: Westview Press, pp. 153–163.

Podgorski, Abelard. 2018. "Wouldn't It Be Nice? Moral Rules and Distant Worlds." *Nous* 52: 279–294.

Portmore, Douglas. 2008. "Are Moral Reasons Morally Overriding?" *Ethical Theory and Moral Practice* 11: 369–388.

Portmore, Douglas. 2019. *Opting for the Best: Oughts and Options.* New York: Oxford University Press.

Portmore, Douglas. forthcoming. "Consequentializing Agent-Centered Restrictions: A Kantsequentialist Approach." *Analytic Philosophy.*

Pummer, Theron. 2016a. "Whether and Where to Give." *Philosophy and Public Affairs* 44: 77–95.

Pummer, Theron. 2016b. "Risky Giving." *The Philosophers' Magazine* 73: 62–70.

Pummer, Theron. 2018. "Spectrum Arguments and Hypersensitivity." *Philosophical Studies* 175: 1729–1744.

Pummer, Theron. 2019. "All or Nothing, But If Not All, Next Best or Nothing." *Journal of Philosophy* 116: 278–291.

Pummer, Theron. 2020. "Review of *The Precipice: Existential Risk and the Future of Humanity.*" *Notre Dame Philosophical Reviews.* https://ndpr.nd.edu/reviews/the-precipice-existential-risk-and-the-future-of-humanity/

Pummer, Theron. 2021. "Impermissible yet Praiseworthy." *Ethics* 131: 697–726.

Pummer, Theron. 2022. "Sorites on What Matters." In *Ethics and Existence: The Legacy of Derek Parfit,* eds. Jeff McMahan, Tim Campbell, James Goodrich, and Ketan Ramakrishnan, Oxford: Oxford University Press, pp. 498–523.

Pummer, Theron. forthcoming. *Hypersensitive Ethics: Much Ado about Nearly Nothing.* Oxford: Oxford University Press.

Pummer, Theron. unpublished. "Lifetime Prerogatives and Moral Offsetting."

Pummer, Theron, and Roger Crisp. 2020. "Rescue and Personal Involvement: A Response to Woollard." *Analysis* 80: 59–66.

Quong, Jonathan. 2009. "Killing in Self-Defense." *Ethics* 119: 507–537.

Quong, Jonathan. 2011. "Left-Libertarianism: Rawlsian not Luck Egalitarian." *Journal of Political Philosophy* 19: 64–89.

Quong, Jonathan. 2020. *The Morality of Defensive Force.* Oxford: Oxford University Press.

Rabenberg, Michael. 2014. "Harm." *Journal of Ethics and Social Philosophy* 8: 1–32.

Rabinowicz, Wlodek. 2012. "Value Relations Revisited." *Economics and Philosophy* 28: 133–164.

Rachels, Stuart. 1998. "Counterexamples to the Transitivity of Better Than." *Australasian Journal of Philosophy* 76: 71–83.

Rawls, John. 1971. *A Theory of Justice*. Cambridge, MA: Harvard University Press.

Ross, Jacob. 2015. "Rethinking the Person-Affecting Principle." *Journal of Moral Philosophy* 12: 428–461.

Ross, W. D. 1930. *The Right and the Good*. Oxford: Oxford University Press.

Rulli, Tina. 2020. "Conditional Obligations." *Social Theory and Practice* 46: 365–390.

Sachs, Benjamin. 2017. *Explaining Right and Wrong: A New Moral Pluralism and Its Implications*. New York: Routledge.

Saunders-Hastings, Emma. 2022. *Private Virtues, Public Vices: Philanthropy and Democratic Equality*. Chicago: University of Chicago Press.

Scanlon, T. M. 1998. *What We Owe to Each Other*. Cambridge, MA: Harvard University Press.

Scanlon, T. M. 2008. *Moral Dimensions: Permissibility, Meaning, Blame*. Cambridge, MA: Harvard University Press.

Scheffler, Samuel. 1982. *The Rejection of Consequentialism: A Philosophical Investigation of the Considerations Underlying Rival Moral Conceptions*. Oxford: Oxford University Press.

Scheffler, Samuel. 2004. "Projects, Relationships, and Reasons." In *Reason and Value: Themes from the Moral Philosophy of Joseph Raz*, ed. R. Jay Wallace, Oxford: Oxford University Press, pp. 247–269.

Scheffler, Samuel. 2018. "Membership and Political Obligation." *Journal of Political Philosophy* 26: 3–23.

Schmidtz, David. 2000. "Islands in a Sea of Obligation: Limits of the Duty to Rescue." *Law and Philosophy* 19: 683–705.

Schoenfield, Miriam. 2016. "Moral Vagueness Is Ontic Vagueness." *Ethics* 126: 257–282.

Schwartz, Thomas. 1972. "Rationality and the Myth of the Maximum." *Nous* 7: 97–117.

Sebo, Jeff, and Laurie Paul. 2019. "Effective Altruism and Transformative Experience." In *Effective Altruism: Philosophical Issues*, eds. Hilary Greaves and Theron Pummer, Oxford: Oxford University Press, pp. 53–68.

Setiya, Kieran. 2014. "Love and the Value of a Life." *Philosophical Review* 123: 251–280.

Setiya, Kieran. forthcoming. "Other People." In *Rethinking the Value of Humanity*, eds. Sarah Buss and Nandi Theunissen, Oxford: Oxford University Press.

Shiffrin, Seana. 1991. "Moral Autonomy and Agent-Centered Options." *Analysis* 51: 244–254.

Shiffrin, Seana. 1999. "Wrongful Life, Procreative Responsibility, and the Significance of Harm." *Legal Theory* 5: 117–148.

Shiffrin, Seana. 2012. "Harm and Its Moral Significance." *Legal Theory* 18: 357–398.

Shue, Henry. 1980. *Basic Rights: Subsistence, Affluence, and U.S. Foreign Policy*. Princeton: Princeton University Press.

Silk, Alex. 2014. "Why 'Ought' Detaches: Or, Why You Ought to Get with My Friends (If You Want to Be My Lover)." *Philosophers' Imprint* 14: 1–16.

Sin, William. 2010. "Trivial Sacrifices, Great Demands." *Journal of Moral Philosophy* 7: 3–15.

Sinclair, Thomas. 2018. "Are We Conditionally Obligated to Be Effective Altruists?" *Philosophy and Public Affairs* 46: 36–59.

Singer, Peter. 1972. "Famine, Affluence, and Morality." *Philosophy and Public Affairs* 1: 229–243.

Singer, Peter. 2005. "Ethics and Intuitions." *Journal of Ethics* 9: 331–352.

Singer, Peter, John McKie, Helga Kuhse, and Jeff Richardson. 1995. "Double Jeopardy and the Use of QALYs in Health Care Allocation." *Journal of Medical Ethics* 21: 144–150.

Skorupski, John. 2010. *The Domain of Reasons*. Oxford: Oxford University Press.

Slavny, Adam, Kai Spiekermann, Holly Lawford-Smith, and David V. Axelsen. 2021. "Directed Reflective Equilibrium: Thought Experiments and How to Use Them." *Journal of Moral Philosophy* 18: 1–25.

Slote, Michael. 1985. *Common-Sense Morality and Consequentialism*. London: Routledge and Kegan Paul.

Smith, Holly. 1991. "Varieties of Moral Worth and Moral Credit." *Ethics* 101: 279–303.

Smith, Patricia. 1990. "The Duty to Rescue and the Slippery Slope Problem." *Social Theory and Practice* 16: 19–41.

Snedegar, Justin. 2017. *Contrastive Reasons*. Oxford: Oxford University Press.

Snowden, James. 2019. "Should We Give to More Than One Charity?" In *Effective Altruism: Philosophical Issues*, eds. Hilary Greaves and Theron Pummer, Oxford: Oxford University Press, pp. 69–79.

Spencer, Jack. 2021. "The Procreative Asymmetry and the Impossibility of Elusive Permission." *Philosophical Studies* 178: 3819–3842.

Sterri, Aksel Braanen, and Ole Martin Moen. 2021. "The Ethics of Emergencies." *Philosophical Studies* 178: 2621–2634.

Stratton-Lake, Philip. 2020. "Intuitionism in Ethics." In *The Stanford Encyclopedia of Philosophy*, ed. Edward Zalta. https://plato.stanford.edu/entries/intuitionism-ethics/

Stroud, Sarah. 2010. "Permissible Partiality, Projects, and Plural Agency." In *Partiality and Impartiality: Morality, Special Relationships, and the Wider World*, eds. Brian Feltham and John Cottingham, Oxford: Oxford University Press, pp. 131–149.

Stroud, Sarah. 2013. "They Can't Take That Away from Me: Restricting the Reach of Morality's Demands." *Oxford Studies in Normative Ethics* 3: 203–234.

Tadros, Victor. 2013. "Controlling Risk." In *Prevention and the Limits of the Criminal Law*, eds. Andrew Ashworth, Lucia Zedner, and Patrick Tomlin, Oxford: Oxford University Press, pp. 133–155.

Taurek, John. 1977. "Should the Numbers Count?" *Philosophy and Public Affairs* 6: 293–316.

Temkin, Larry. 1993. *Inequality*. Oxford: Oxford University Press.

Temkin, Larry. 2012. *Rethinking the Good: Moral Ideals and the Nature of Practical Reasoning*. New York: Oxford University Press.

Temkin, Larry. 2019. "Being Good in a World of Need: Some Empirical Worries and an Uncomfortable Philosophical Possibility." *Journal of Practical Ethics* 7: 1–24.

Temkin, Larry. 2022. *Being Good in a World of Need*. New York: Oxford University Press.

Thoma, Johanna. 2019. "Risk Aversion and the Long Run." *Ethics* 129: 230–253.

Thomson, Jordan. 2020. "Poverty and the Peril of Particulars." *Journal of Applied Philosophy* 37: 661–677.

Thomson, Jordan. 2021. "Relief from Rescue." *Philosophical Studies*, 179: 1221–1239. https://doi.org/10.1007/s11098-021-01705-1

Thomson, Judith. 1971. "A Defense of Abortion." *Philosophy and Public Affairs* 1: 47–66.

Thomson, Judith. 1990. *The Realm of Rights*. Cambridge, MA: Harvard University Press.

Timmerman, Travis. 2015. "Sometimes There Is Nothing Wrong with Letting a Child Drown." *Analysis* 75: 204–212.

Timmerman, Travis. 2019. "Effective Altruism's Underspecification Problem." In *Effective Altruism: Philosophical Issues*, eds. Hilary Greaves and Theron Pummer, Oxford: Oxford University Press, pp. 166–183.

Timmerman, Travis, and Yishai Cohen. 2020. "Actualism and Possibilism in Ethics." In *The Stanford Encyclopedia of Philosophy*, ed. Edward Zalta. https://plato.stanford.edu/entries/actualism-possibilism-ethics/

Timmermann, Jens. 2004. "The Individualist Lottery: How People Count, but Not Their Numbers." *Analysis* 64: 106–112.

Timmermann, Jens. 2005. "Good but Not Required?—Assessing the Demands of Kantian Ethics." *Journal of Moral Philosophy* 2: 9–27.

Todd, Patrick. 2019. "A Unified Account of the Moral Standing to Blame." *Nous* 53: 347–374.

Tucker, Chris. unpublished. "The All or Nothing Ranking Reversal and the Unity of Morality."

Unger, Peter. 1996. *Living High and Letting Die: Our Illusion of Innocence*. New York: Oxford University Press.

Urmson, James. 1958. "Saints and Heroes." In *Essays in Moral Philosophy*, ed. A. I. Melden, Seattle: University of Washington Press, pp. 198–216.

Višak, Tatjana, and Robert Garner. 2015. *The Ethics of Killing Animals*. Oxford: Oxford University Press.

Voorhoeve, Alex. 2014. "How Should We Aggregate Competing Claims?" *Ethics* 125: 64–87.

Walden, Kenneth. 2014. "The Aid That Leaves Something to Chance." *Ethics* 124: 231–241.

Wallace, R. Jay. 2010. "Hypocrisy, Moral Address, and the Equal Standing of Persons." *Philosophy and Public Affairs* 38: 307–341.

Wasserman, David, and Alan Strudler. 2003. "Can a Nonconsequentialist Count Lives?" *Philosophy and Public Affairs* 31: 71–94.

Wenar, Leif. 2011. "Poverty Is No Pond: Challenges for the Affluent." In *Giving Well: The Ethics of Philanthropy*, eds. Patricia Illingworth, Thomas Pogge, and Leif Wenar, New York: Oxford University Press, pp. 104–132.

White, Stephen. 2021. "Self-Prediction in Practical Reasoning: Its Role and Limits." *Nous* 55: 825–841.

Williams, Bernard. 1973. *Utilitarianism: For and Against*. Cambridge: Cambridge University Press.

Woollard, Fiona. 2014. "The New Problem of Numbers in Morality." *Ethical Theory and Moral Practice* 17: 631–641.

Woollard, Fiona. 2015. *Doing and Allowing Harm*. Oxford: Oxford University Press.

Woollard, Fiona. 2016. "*Dimensions of Demandingness.*" *Proceedings of the Aristotelian Society* 116: 89–106.

Woollard, Fiona. 2019. "Barry and Øverland on Doing, Allowing and Enabling Harm." *Ethics and Global Politics* 12: 43–51.

Zimmerman, Michael. 1988. *An Essay on Moral Responsibility*. Totowa: Rowman and Littlefield.

INDEX

For the benefit of digital users, indexed terms that span two pages (e.g., 52–53) may, on occasion, appear on only one of those pages.